The book primarily attempts to introduce those whose mother tongue is not Hindi to learning of Hindi by the most natural and the simplest method. It adopts the scientific approach, introducing alphabets, words, sentences in that order and application of these in the most common situations of daily life. Situational sentences and conversational sentences selected for the book reflect the maximum possible commonness of Indian languages and Indian culture.

LEARN HINDI IN 30 DAYS THROUGH ENGLISH

Chief Editor
Krishna Gopal Vikal

Editor : Hindi Edition
Amitabh Dhingra

FUSION BOOKS

ISBN : 81-288-1125-8

Published by : **Fusion Books**
X-30, Okhla Industrial Area, Phase-II
New Delhi-110020
Phone : 011-41611861-65, 40712100
Fax : 011-41611866
E-mail : sales@dpb.in
Website : www.dpb.in
Edition : 2011
Printed by : India Offset Pvt. Ltd., X-36, Okhla-II, New Delhi

---

LEARN HINDI IN 30 DAYS THROUGH ENGLISH
by : Krishna Gopal Vikal

Dedicated to

Dr. Ashok Ramchandra Kelkar
Renonw Philologist of India
whose advice was the source of inspiration

A WORD FROM THE PUBLISHER

We are glad to announce that with a view to strengthening the unity of our country, we shall be publishing the book-series 'LEARN THE NATIONAL LANGUAGES' to enable people of this country to learn any Indian language other than his mother tongue, through the medium of English.

Each book of the series will be divided in five parts. The first two parts will cover the basic knowledge about the language concerned and the rest will be devoted to conversational aspects and practical application of the language.

The books will be prepared under the able guidance of the well-known author and editor of several books, Shri Krishna Gopal Vikal, who is the chief editor of this book and he will be assisted by Shri Amitabh Dhingra. Format and scheme of all books will be the same as that of this book and each book will be prepared in close consultation with the topmost linguists of the language concerned.

We hope this series will bring together the people of various parts of our country promoting mutual understanding and fostering national unity. We hereby present the first book 'Diamond Hindi Learning and Speaking Course'.

– Publisher

FORWORD

The greatest sensation of life is to learn a language. One has to closely watch a child going through this experience, to be convinced of this. Every time he learn a new word or construction from mother, father or other relatives, his heart is filled with wonder, excitement, thrill and creative urge and he toys with its various forms and tones bringing into play all the creative forces within him.

To learn a new language is to re-enter this wonderful experience of life, opening infinite opportunities for creative action. Besides, in a fast expanding world transcending all barriers of colour, caste, religion and language, a new language is an essential tool of life.

The book primarily attempts to introduce those whose mother tongue is not Hindi to learning of Hindi by the most natural and the simplest method. It adopts the scientific approach, introducing alphabets, words, sentences in that order and application of these in the most common situations of daily life. Situational sentences and conversational sentences selected for the book reflect the maximum possible commonness of Indian languages and Indian culture. The purpose is that the learner during the process of learning should be sufficiently equipped to converse and transact with a very vast section of Hindi speaking people throughout India and abroad.

Since Hindi is mother-tounge of about 30 crores of people and is spoken or understood by another 20 crores or so and since it is the principal link language of the greatest democracy of the world, acquaintance with this not only enables one to establish a direct communication with millions of people, thereby promoting his career prospects and business interests, but also gives him the spiritual satisfaction of belonging to a vast family.

The book can also be helpful to foreigners who are on visit to India as tourists, scholars, diplomats and businessmen as it would enable them to move about in different parts of the country transending the language barriers.

We hope the book will serve the purpose. It will be popular among the youngsters as well as the serious language learner. We are grateful to Shri Narendra Kumar, Director of Diamomd Pocket Books, who has wisely taken special initiative to bring out this very useful series. We also express out gratitute to the persons concerned with proof-reading, printing and production of the book.

– Krishna Gopal Vikal
Amitabh Dhingra

CONTENTS

PART 1
ALPHABET

IST STEP पहली सीढ़ी

WELCOME YOU ALL
आप सबका स्वागत है

This book is in your hands.

It shows that you intend to learn Hindi. It is a matter of pleasure to us.

Of all the languages of India, Hindi is undoubtedly the most widely spoken. It is probably one of the three greatest spoken languages (English, Chinese and Hindi) of the world. It is a language which has vast and rich literature.

We welcome you all for your praiseworthy enthusiasm and fully assure you for the success. You will move on continually–step by step until you reach your destination. Let us start our journey.

Sentences of Greetings in Conversation

In Hindi, there are no separate clauses for timely salutations as in English, e.g., 'Good morning', 'Good evening', 'Good night' etc. We say every time we meet नमस्कार (Namaskar) or नमस्ते (Namaste), etc. The people of different religions and faiths alternatively use their own wordings also, e.g., जय राम जी की! सत् श्री अकाल ! सलाम आलेकुम, etc.'

***While meeting* मिलने पर**

Good morning, Sir!	नमस्कार, श्रीमान्!	Namaskār, shrīmān!

Good morning! Madam	नमस्कार, महोदया!	Namaskār, Mahodayā!
Good afternoon, my friend!	नमस्ते, मित्र!	Namaste, mitra!
Good afternoon, my brother!	नमस्ते, भाई!	Namaste, bhāī!
Good evening, boss!	नमस्कार, महोदय!	Namaskār, mahodayā!
Good evening my, comrade!	नमस्ते, साथी!	Namaste, Sāthi!
Good night, my sister!	शुभ रात्रि, बहन!	Suhubh rātrī, bahin!

***While departing* विदा होने पर**

Good bye, my child!	विदा, मेरे बच्चे!	Vidā, mere bachache!
Bye bye!	अच्छा विदा!	Achchha vidā!
Ta-Ta!	अलविदा!	Alvidā !
Good bye!	अलविदा!	Alvidā !

***Good wishes* शुभ कामनाएँ**

Happy Diwali!	दीवाली शुभ हो!	Diwāli shubh ho!
Happy Id!	ईद मुबारक!	Id mubarak!
Happy Guru parva!	गुरुपर्व की बधाई!	Gurpurva ki badhāī!
Happ X-mas!	क्रिसमस पर बधाई!	Krismas par badhāī!

REMARKABLE उल्लेखनीय

In Hindi, all Indians can say नमस्कार (Namaskār) or नमस्ते (Namaste) in salutations. To show his absolute faith in his religion and creed etc., a Muslim will say सलाम आलेकुम (Salām ālekum), a Sikh सत् श्री अकाल (Sat shri akal), a Nationalist जय हिंद (Jai Hind) & a Humanist जय जगत् (Jai jagat).

2ND STEP दूसरी सीढ़ी

ALPHABET
वर्णमाला

Hindī language is written in Devnāgarī script which is common with Sanskrit, Marathi and Nepālī.

Hindi alphabet consists of vowels and consonants which are 11 and 35 respectively.

Here are going to deal with vowels.

VOWELS स्वर

अ	आ	इ	ई	उ	ऊ	ऋ
a	ā	i	ī	u	ū	ri
ए	ऐ	ओ	औ	अं	अः	
e	ai	o	au	aṅ	aḥ	

Recognise and pronounce—

उ	ऊ	अ	आ
ओ	औ	अं	अः
इ	ई		ऋ
ए	ऐ		

1. The vowels अ आ ओ औ अं अः were also written as अ आ ओ औ अं अः respectively, but in standardized Devnagari, these forms are excluded. The Hindi learners should keep it in mind.

2. In Hindi, there are two classes of vowels:

(i) Short (hrasva ह्रस्व) and (ii) long (sandhi संधि) vowels

(i) **Short vowels (ह्रस्व स्वर):**

अ	इ	उ	ऋ
a	i	u	ṛi

(ii) **Long vowels (Sandhi swar संधि-स्वर)**

आ	ई	ऊ	ए	ऐ	ओ	औ
ā	ī	ū	e	ai	o	au

3. Short vowels are to be pronounced short and long vowels, long. Let us learn how to pronounce the vowels.

Letter	*Pronunciation*	*Remarks*
अ	(Short) a	sounds like short 'a' as in **sub**.
आ	(long) ā	sounds like long 'ā' as in **far**.
इ	(short) i	sounds like short 'i' as in **is**.
ई	(long) ī	sounds like long 'ī' as in **meet**.
उ	(short) u	sounds like long 'ī' as in **put**.
ऊ	(long) ū	sounds like long 'ū' as in **wool**.
ऋ	(short) rī	sounds like 'ri' as in **rib**.
ए	(long) e	sounds like 'e', as in **say**.
ऐ	(diphthong) ai	sounds like 'ai' as in **ass**.
ओ	(long) o	sounds like 'o' as in **role**.
औ	(diphthong) au	sounds like 'an' as in **shout**.
अं	(long) aṅ	sounds like 'un' as in **hunger**.
अ:	(long) ah	sounds like 'h' as in **ah**.

REMARKABLE उल्लेखनीय

* ऋ is different from रि in pronunciation. Actually ऋ is used in writing only तत्सम or संस्कृत words. It is not accepted as a vowel within the Hindi phonetic set-up.
* अ, (अँ), अ: are not vowels, but semi-consonants (अयोगवाह). For the sake of convenience, these are put among vowels.

3RD STEP तीसरी सीढ़ी

CONSONANTS
व्यंजन

As we know, there are 35 consonants in Hindi. Some are peculiar to Hindi, and they have no equivalent in English.

The consonants reproduced below in the manner in which they are generally found in Hindi books.

क	ख	ग	घ	ङ	च	छ	ज	झ	ञ
ka	**kha**	**gā**	**gha**	**ṅa**	**cha**	**chha**	**ja**	**jha**	**ṅa**
ट	ठ	ड	ढ	ण	त	थ	द	ध	व
ṭa	**ṭh**	**ḍa**	**ḍha**	**ṇa**	**ta**	**tha**	**da**	**dha**	**na**
प	फ	ब	भ	म		य	र	ल	व
pa	**pha**	**ba**	**bha**	**ma**		**ya**	**ra**	**la**	**va**
श	ष	स	ह					ड़	ढ़
sha	**ṣha**	**sa**	**ha**					**ṛa**	**ṛha**

1. अ (a) is incorporated in every consonant sound, but while pronouncing words this final vowel sound is often dropped. As—'बचत' (Bachata) is pronounced like 'बचत्' (Bachat).
2. If any consonant is to be written where the vowel अ is not blended with it, a sign हल् (्) is used. As पश्चात् (Pashchāt).

3. The consonants without अ or any other vowel can be written as , are shown below—

क् + अ = क, च् + आ = चा, त् + अ = त, प् + आ = पा etc.

4. The letters छ झ ण ल and श were also written as छ, झ, ण, ल and श respectively; but in standardized Devnāgari, later forms are excluded.

5. The letters ख, ध, भ and त्र are written as ख, ध, भ and त्र respectively; so both the forms should be known.

Identify and pronounce—

ग	म	भ	र	स	ख	श	व	ब	क
घ	ध	ड	ड	ड़	ढ़	ढ	ट	ण	ठ
त	न	य	थ	च	ज	छ	द	फ	प
ल	ष	स	श	ह					

Kinds of Consonants

6. Basically the consonants are of three kinds— (i) स्पर्श, (ii) अंतस्थ, and (iii) ऊष्म।

From क to म—the first 25 consonants are known as स्पर्श व्यंजन। Among the remaining eight consonants, the first four, i.e., य, र, ल, व are अंतस्थ व्यंजन and the later four श, ष, स, ह are ऊष्म व्यंजन।

Pronunciation of consonants

7. Let us kow how to pronounce consonants.

Letter	***Pronunciation***	***Remarks***
क	ka	k, as in **king.**
ख	kha	ck-h, as in **blaack-hole** (but as a single sound)
ग	ga	g, as in **gate.**
घ	gha	gh, as in **ghost.**
ङ	ṅa	ng, as in **long.**

च	cha	ch, as in **such.**
छ	chha	ch-h, as in **church-hill** (as a single sound)
ज	ja	j, as in **jug.**
झ	jha	ge-h, as in **large-hill** (as a single sound)
ञ	ṅa	nya, as **lanyard** (as a single sound).
ट	ṭa	t, as in **tank.**
ठ	ṭha	t-h, as in **short-hand** (as a single sound).
ड	ḍa	d, as in **day.**
ढ	ḍha	d-h, as in **sand-hill** (as a single sound).
ण	ṇa	n, as in **band**.
त	ta	t (softer than English **t:** similar to Italian pronunciation) as Hindi word तट (tat).
थ	tha	th, as in **thumb.**
द	da	id, as in **thus.**
ध	dha	**aspirated** द, not found in English. As in Hindi word **Dharma.**
न	na	n, as in **not.**
प	pa	p, as in **pot.**
फ	pha	ph, as a **loop hole** (as a single sound).
ब	ba	b, as in **bat.**
भ	bha	bh, as in **sub-house** (as a single sound).
म	ma	m, as in **man.**
य	ya	y, as in **young.**
र	ra	r, nearly as in **rate.**
ल	la	l, as in **land.**
व	va	v or w, as in **vote** or **wine.**
श	sha	sh, as in **shut.**

ष	ṣa	not found in English. Actually in Hindi ष differs little from श. As in Hindi word धनुष
स	sa	s, as in **some.**
ह	ha	h, as in **has.**
ड़	ṛa	r, as in Hindi word जड़। As American pronounce r in **very.**
ढ़	ṛha	as in Hindi word गढ़ & पढ़. It is not found in English language.

Some important points to be remembered

1. ङ, ञ, ण, ड़ or ढ़ never come in the beginning of a word.
2. The use of ङ & ञ has almost disappeared from modern Hindi.
3. ख, घ, छ, झ, ठ, ढ, ण, ध, फ, भ and ष are the consonants, which are peculiar to Hindi, and in fact, they have no equivalent in English. The accurate pronunciation of above letters can only be mastered through the practice.

4TH STEP चौथी सीढ़ी

HOW TO WRITE ALPHABET

1. Hindi is written in Devnāgarī script. The script is written from left to right as the roman script. But it has headline above the letters.
2. How to begin writing is clearly indicated by numbers 1, 2, 3, 4, 5. Start writting from No. 1, 2, 3 and so on. You will find, you are on the right path.

Let us begin to write vowels and consonants respectively.

VOWELS स्वर

अ	आ	इ
ई	उ	ऊ
ऋ	ए	ऐ
ओ	औ	अं
	अः	

CONSONANTS व्यंजन

क	ख	ग	घ
ड़	च	छ	ज
झ	ञ	ट	ठ
ड	ढ	ण	त
थ	द	ध	न
प	फ	ब	भ
म	य	र	ल
व	श	ष	स
ह	क्ष	त्र	ज्ञ
	ड़	ढ़	

REMARKABLE उल्लेखनीय

1. In this chapter, these are all the standardized Devnāgarī letters. These must be learnt.
2. Devnāgarī script is written from left to right. It has headline above the letters.
3. क्ष, त्र, ज्ञ are not consonants; these are conjuncts.
4. The strokes for every letter are marked. Try to write accordingly.

5TH STEP पांचवीं सीढ़ी

VOWELS & THEIR ABBREVIATED FORMS
स्वर एवं उनकी मात्राएँ

In Devnāgarī script, there are two forms of vowels—(i) Syllabic forms, and (ii) Abbreviated forms. Here are syllabic forms and abbreviated forms of Hindi vowels—

Syllabic Forms : अ आ इ ई उ ऊ ऋ ए ऐ ओ औ अं अः

Abbreviated Forms : – ा ि ी ु ू ृ े ै ो ौ

1. (i) Syllabic forms of vowels are used separately. As—

आ (ā) Come आओ (āo) Come आइए (āiye) Please come

(ii) Abbreviated forms of vowels are used combined with preceding consonants characters are as follow:

(a) ा ी ो ौ follow the consonant.

(b) ि precedes it.

(c) ु ू ृ are subscripts.

(d) े ै are subscripts.

These are abbreviated forms of vowels, called mātrās (मात्राएं)

Combination of Abbreviated Forms of Vowels (Mātrās) with Consonants

2. Let us combine the intra-syllabic forms of all vowels (मात्राएँ) with consonants **क् (K)** They are called बारहखड़ी (bārah kharī)

क	का	कि	की	कु	कू	कृ	के	कै	को	कौ	कं	कः
ka	kā	ki	kī	ku	kū	kṛ	ke	kai	ko	kau	kam	kaḥ

Thus the Matrās can be combined with all preceding consonants. Now we elaborate this combination.

ख	खा	खि	खी	खु	खू	खृ	खे	खे	खो	खौ	खं	खः
kha	khā	khi	khī	khu	khū	khṛ	khe	khai	kho	khau	kham	khaḥ
ग	गा	गि	गी	गु	गू	गृ	गे	गै	गो	गौ	गं	गः
ga	gā	gi	gī	gu	gū	gṛ	ge	gai	go	gau	gam	gaḥ
घ	घा	घि	घी	घु	घू	घृ	घे	घै	घो	घौ	घं	घः
gha	ghā	ghi	ghī	ghu	ghū	ghṛ	ghe	ghai	gho	ghau	ghau	ghaḥ
च	चा	चि	ची	चु	चू	चृ	चे	चै	चो	चौ	चं	चः
cha	chā	chi	chī	chu	chū	chṛ	che	chai	cho	chau	cham	chaḥ
ट	टा	टि	टी	टु	टू	टृ	टे	टै	टो	टौ	टं	टः
ta	tā	ti	tī	tu	tū	tṛ	te	tai	to	tau	tam	taḥ
त	ता	ति	ती	तु	तू	तृ	ते	तै	तो	तौ	तं	तः
ta	tā	ti	tī	tu	tū	tṛ	te	tai	to	tau	tam	taḥ
प	पा	पि	पी	पु	पू	पृ	पे	पै	पो	पौ	पं	पः
pa	pā	pi	pī	pu	pū	pṛ	pe	pai	po	pau	pam	paḥ
य	या	यि	यी	यु	यू	यृ	ये	यै	यो	यौ	यं	यः
ya	yā	yi	yī	yu	yū	yṛ	ye	yai	yo	yau	yam	yaḥ
र	रा	रि	री	रु	रू	–	रे	रै	रो	रौ	रं	रः
ra	rā	ri	rī	ru	rū	–	re	rai	ro	rau	ram	raḥ
ल	ला	लि	ली	लु	लू	लृ	ले	लै	लो	लौ	लं	लः
la	lā	li	lī	lu	lū	lṛ	le	lai	lo	lau	lam	laḥ
व	वा	वि	वी	वु	वू	वृ	वे	वै	वो	वौ	वं	वः
va	vā	vi	vī	vu	vū	vṛ	ve	vai	vo	vau	vam	vaḥ
श	शा	शि	शी	शु	शू	शृ	शे	शै	शो	शौ	शं	शः
sha	shā	shi	shḥ	shu	shū	shṛ	she	shai	sho	shau	sham	shaḥ

स	सा	सि	सी	सु	सू	सृ	से	सै	सो	सौ	सं	सः
sa	sā	si	sī	su	sū	sṛ	se	sai	so	sau	sam	saḥ
ह	हा	हि	ही	हु	हू	हृ	हे	है	हो	हौ	हं	हः
ha	hā	hi	hī	hu	hū	hṛ	he	hai	ho	hau	ham	haḥ

etc. आदि-आदि

3. Vowels–signs (Mātrās) are used in the same way with all the consonants excepting उ and ऊ with र as—

   र् + उ = रु   र् + ऊ = रू

Making the words combining vowels with consonants

Let us combine the vowels with consonants and make words. Thus we shall attain knowledge of various sounds of Hindi language and learn the meaning of many words.

(i) Combining the vowel आ *(ā) with consonants*

Combination of आ will be like-wise—

काम **kām,** work — नाम **nām,** name

माता **mātā,** mother — खाना **khānā,** food

बड़ा **baṛā,** big — पता **patā,** address

जागना **jāgnā,** to rise — भागना **bhāgnā,** to run

गहना **gahnā,** ornament — झरना **jharnā,** fountain

(ii) Combining the vowel इ *(i) with consonants*

When joined to a consonant, original vowel इ gives place to its sign which is used before the consonants concerned.

दिन **din,** day — सिर **sir,** head

पिता **pitā,** father — बिना **bina,** without

यदि **yadi,** if — गति **gati,** speed

मित्र **mitra,** friend — चित्र **chitra,** picture

शनिवार **shanivar,** Saturday — रविवार **ravivar,** Sunday

(iii) Combining the vowel ई *(ī) with consonants*

Combination of ई (i) will be like-wise—

ठीक **ṭhik,** right

गीत **gīt,** song

गरीब **garib,** poor

शरीर **sharār,** body

दीवार **dīvār,** wall

बीमार **bīmār,** ill

गरमी **garmī,** summer

सर्दी **sardī,** winter

(iv) Combining the vowel उ (u) with consonants

When उ (u) or ऊ (ū) is to be blended with a consonant except र its abbreviated form is put under the consonant.

उ (u)

गुण **gun,** quality

सुन **sun,** to hear

गुलाब **gulāb,** rose

चुनाव **chunāv,** election

पशु **pashu,** animal

वायु **vāyu,** air

ऊ (u)

झूठ **jhūth,** lie

दूध **dūdh,** milk

फूल **phūl,** flower

भूल **bhūl,** mistake

चाकू **chakū,** knife

डाकू **dakū,** dacoit

But when उ (u) or ऊ (u) is to be blended with र, its abbreviated form (mātra मात्रा) is put the middle. Thus—

उ (u)

रुपया **rupayā,** rupee

रुपहला **rupahlā,** silvery

रुकना **ruknā,** to stop

रुचि **ruchi,** interest

ऊ (ū)

शुरू **shurū,** begin

रूप **rūp,** shape, beauty

रूठना **rūthnā,** to be displeased

रूखा **rūkhā,** rough

(v) Combining the vowel ऋ (ṛi) with consonants

The pronunciation of ऋ – is very near to the pronunciation of 'ri' in English word **'bridge'.** Its pronunciation is somewhere between अ & इ. Actually a bit near to इ. But in modern Hindi, it is usually pronounced as कृपा (kripā).

There are some examples in which the combination of ऋ with different consonants can be seen.

कृपा **kripā,** kindness

घृणा **ghrinā,** hatred

कृषि **krishi,** agriculture

गृह **grih,** home

पृथक् **prithak,** separate

कृपण **kripaṇ,** miser

(vi) Combining the vowel ए *(e) or* ऐ *(ai) with consonants*

ए (e)

देश **desh,** country

खेत **khet,** field

मुझे **mujhe,** to me

उसे **use,** to him or her

सेवा **sevā,** service

सेना **senā,** army

लेटना **letnā,** to lay down

बेंचना **bechnā,** to sell

ऐ (aī)

कैसे **kaise,** how

वैसे **vaise,** in that way

वैर **vair,** enmity

गैर **gair,** other

मैला **mailā,** dirty

थैला **thailā,** bag

दैनिक **dainik,** daily

सैनिक **sainik,** doldier

(vii) Combining the vowel ओ *(o) or* औ *(au) with consonants*

ओ (o)

चोर **chor,** thief

मोर **mor,** peacock

दोष **doṣ,** fault

कोष **koṣ,** treasure

तोड़ना **toṛnā,** to break

जोड़ना **joṛnā,** to unite

भोजन **bhojan,** food

बोतल **botal,** bottle

औ (au)

कौन **kaun,** who

मौन **maun,** silence

नौकर **naukar,** servant

चौथा **chauthā,** fourth

कौआ **kauā,** crow

हौआ **hauā,** bogey.

मौसम **mausam,** weather

चौड़ा **chauṛā,** wide

(viii) Combining the semi-vowels [अयोगवाह] *with consonants*

In Hindi, there are three अयोगवाह (semi-vowels)—

(i) अनुस्वार (Anuswar)—It is placed above the vowel (e.g., अंग) or consonant + vowel, after which it is pronounced (e.g., मंद).

(ii) विसर्ग (Visarga)—It is placed after the vowel or consonant + vowel (e.g., निःसंदेह, दुःख, etc.). It is used with the Sanskrit words.

(iii) अनुनासिक (Anunasik)—It is half nasal sound. It is called chandrabinbu (चंद्रबिंदु) too.

(a) It is used only when there is no vowel-sign on the top of a letter; as— आँख, ऊँट etc.

(b) But when there is any vowel-sign on the top of a letter (ि, ी, े, ै, ो, ौ) the dot (.) only is used. As– हमें, हैं, हों etc.

Let us have some more words.

अनुस्वार (ं)

अंक **aṅka,** number	अंग **aṅga,** body
अंश **aṅshā,** part	सिंह **siṅha,** lion

विसर्ग (:)

दुःख **duḥkha,** sorrow	निःसंकोच **niḥsankoch,** unhesitating
पुनः **punaḥ,** again	दुःसह **duhsaḥ,** unbearable

अनुनासिक (ँ)

हँसी **han:sī,** laugh	हूँ **hūn:,** am
आँख **ān:kh,** eye	कहाँ **kahan:,** where

REMARKABLE उल्लेखनीय

1. The abbreviated form of vowel इ (ि) is put before the concerned consonant.
2. The vowel-signs (मात्राएं) are used in the same way with all the consonants except उ & ऊ with र as—
   र + उ = रु   र + ऊ = रू
3. There are much difference among हस, हँस and हंस। हस is un-nasal word, हँस is half-nasal and हंस is nasal word.
4. Mostly the visarga is used in Sanskrit words, as in दुःख, निःसंदेह, etc.

6TH STEP छठी सीढ़ी

CONJUNCTS
संयुक्त वर्ण

क्ष त्र ज्ञ These are three additional letters, which are conjunctures of two consonants and one vowel. Thus they are called conjuncts.

These conjuncts can be separated in this way—

क्ष = क् + ष + अ	kṣa : As in—कक्षा **kakṣā**, class
त्र = त् + र + अ	tra : As in—पत्र **patrā**, letter
ज्ञ = ज् + ञ् + अ	jṅa : As in—ज्ञान **jṅān** or **gyān,** knowledge

संयुक्त वर्ण- When two or more consonants have no vowel between them and they are pronounced together, are called conjuncts.

As— ग् + व = ग्व; द् + द = द्द; फ् + त = फ्त; क् + र = क्र; ट् + ट = ट्ट

The consonants may be divided into five groups for making conjuncts:

(a) पाई वाले व्यंजन (Consonants ending in a vertical line) as— ग् = ग।

(b) खूँटीधारी पाई वाले व्यंजन (Consonants of group 'a' having curve on the right), as— क् = क ।

(c) बिना पाई वाले व्यंजन, जो कि संयुक्ताक्षर के रूप में ऊपर-नीचे लिखे जाते हैं (Consonants not ending in vertical line, which are formed by writing the second one just below the first) As— द् + ध = द्ध

(d) बिना पाई वाले व्यंजन, जो कि संयुक्ताक्षर के रूप में अलग-अलग पहले व्यंजन में हल् लगाकर लिखे जाते हैं (Consonants not ending in vertical line, which are formed by writing the first-one with a Hal-mark) As— ट् + ठ = ट्ठ।

(e) संयुक्ताक्षरों के अपवाद रूप (Exceptional forms of conjuncts) As— र् + क = र्क; ड् + र = ड्र; द् + म = द्म; श् + र् = श्र।

In this group, there are some irregular conjuncts which do not follow any rule.

Now we shall see the conjuncts into the aforesaid groups.

***Group one* पाई वाले व्यंजन**

ग्ग	ग्घ	घ्य	च्च	च्छ	ज्व
त्थ	घ्य	न्य	प्व	ब्य	भ्य
म्य	ल्य	व्य	श्क	ष्य	स्व

***Group two* खूँटीधारी पाई वाले व्यंजन**

क् + य = क्‍य — क्य, क्व, क्त, क्ल

फ् + त = फ्‍त — फ्त, फ्य, फ्व, फ्न

क् + क = क्क, फ् + क = फ्क

***Group three* बिना पाई व्यंजन (ऊपर-नीचे लिखे जाने वाले)**

द् + द = द्द, द् + ध = द्ध, ह् + र = ह्र

द् + व = द्व, ट् + र = ट्र, ड् + र = ड्र

***Group four* बिना पाई व्यंजन (अलग-अगल लिखे जाने वाले)**

ट् + ट = ट्ट, ट् + ठ = ट्ठ

ड् + ड = ड्ड, ढ् + य = ढ्य

***Group five* संयुक्ताक्षरों के अपवाद रूप**

(i) with र

क् + र = क्र/ ग्र, घ्र, ज्र, झ्र

त् + र = त्र/ त्र, द्र, ध्र

प् + र = प्र/ फ्र, ब्र, भ्र, म्र

श् + र = श्र/ व्र, स्र

(ii) र् with other consonants

र् + क = र्क, र्ख, र्ग, र्घ, र्च

र् + छ = र्छ, र्ज, र्ट, र्ठ, र्ड

र् + ण = र्ण, र्त, र्थ, र्द, र्ध

र् + न = र्न, र्प, र्फ, र्ब, र्भ

र् + म = र्म, र्य, र्व, र्ल, र्श

र् + ष = र्ष, र्स, र्ह

(iii) ह् with य, म, न

ह् + म = ह्म, or ह्‌म

ह् + य = ह्य, or ह्‌य

ह् + न = ह्न, or ह्‌न

ह् + व = ह्व, or ह्‌व

द् + म = द्म, or द्‌म

द् + य = द्य, or द्‌य

(iv) क्ष, त्र, ज्ञ

क् + ष = क्ष (कक्षा)

त् + र = त्र or त्र (पत्र)

ज् + ञ = ज्ञ (ज्ञानी)

Let us learn some words constituted with various conjuncts.

(क) भक्ति **bhakti,** devotion, शक्ति **shakti,** power

(ख) मुख्य **mukhya,** chief, संख्या **sankhya,** number

(स्) उपस्थित **upasthit,** present स्थिति **sthiti,** position

(ग्) योग्य **yogya,** able, ग्यारह **gyārah,** eleven

(द्) विद्या **vidyā,** education, द्वारा **dvārā,** by, through

(त्) यत्न **yatna,** effort, सत्य **satya,** truth

(प्) प्यार **pyār,** love, प्यास **pyās,** thirst

(न्) न्याय **nyāy,** justice, अन्य **anya,** other

(च) बच्चा **bachchā,** child (ज्) लज्जा **lajjā,** shame

(ट्) खट्टा **khattā,** sour

(ड) अड्डा **addā,** stoppage

(ल्) बिल्ली **billi,** cat

(ण्) पुण्य **punya,** virtue

(र्) कार्य **kārya,** work,

अर्थ **artha,** meanings,

वर्षा **varṣā,** rain,

शर्म **sharma,** shame

वर्ष **varṣā,** year

कार्यालय **kāryiālay,** office

(-र) प्रकाश **prakāsh,** light,

क्रम **kram,** series,

ड्रामा **drāmā,** drama,

ग्राम **grām,** village,

श्रम **shram,** labour,

राष्ट्र **rāṣtra,** nation

REMARKABLE उल्लेखनीय

1. क्ष, त्र, ज्ञ are additional letters. They are conjuncts.
2. त्र, क्र, द्म, ह्म, ह्न, श्र & द्य are alternatively written as त्र, क्र, द्म, ह्म, ह्न श & द्य।
3. क्र means that the first consonant क्र is हल् (without vowel) र्क means that the first consonant र् is हल् (without vowel). Thus: ट्र means that the first consonant ट् is हल् (without vowel) Learn it.
4. The usage of ङ्, ञ, ण्, न्, म् in the words अंङ्ग, अञ्चल, दण्ड, अन्त, कम्पन, etc., has been excluded from modern Hindi language. Now अनुस्वार (Anuswar) is put instead of them. As— अंक, अंचल, दंड, अंत, कंपन etc.

7TH STEP सातवीं सीढ़ी

THE PARTS OF SPEECH
शब्द के भेद

1. A sentence consits of two parts—उद्देश्य (Subject) and विधेय (Predicate) उद्देश्य is that about which something has been said in the sentence. विधेय is what has been said about it.

   Both the उद्देश्य and the विधेय may consist of more than one word. Thus, every word in a sentence performs a definite function.

2. There are eight categories of classes of words which are called 'Parts of Speech'. They are—

1.	संज्ञा (Noun)	5.	क्रिया-विशेषण (Adverb)
2.	सर्वनाम (Pronoun)	6.	संबंध-बोधक (Post-position)
3.	विशेषण (Adjective)	7.	योजक (Conjunction)
4.	क्रिया (Verb)	8.	विस्मयादिबोधक (Exclamation)

The first four are विकारी (Declinable), and second four are अविकारी (Indeclinable).

Now, read carefully the following sentence—

ओह! छोटे भाई और बहन ने मुझे कमरे के अंदर हौले-हौले बताया।

Oh! Younger brother and sister told me quietly in the room.

In the above sentence—

'ओह! छोटे भाई और बहन ने' is उद्देश्य (subject)

and—

'मुझे कमरे के अंदर हौले-हौले बताया' is विधेय (predicate).

Let us explain every word of this sentence in detail grammaticaly and try to test each word what part of speech it is.

(1) ओह (oh) — Exclamation[8]

(2) छोटे (younger) —Adjective[3]

(3) भाई (brother) — Noun[1]

(4) और (and) — Conjuction[7]

(5) बहन ने (sister) — Noun[1]

(6) मुझे (to me) — Pronoun[2]

(7) (कमरे) के अंदर [inside (the room)] — Post-position[6]

(8) हौले-हौले (quietly) — Adverb[5]

(9) बताया (told) — Verb[4]

Thus, we learn the role of every parts of speech. In the following chapters, we shall explain every constitution of sentence very briefly.

THE PARTS OF SPEECH
शब्द के भेद

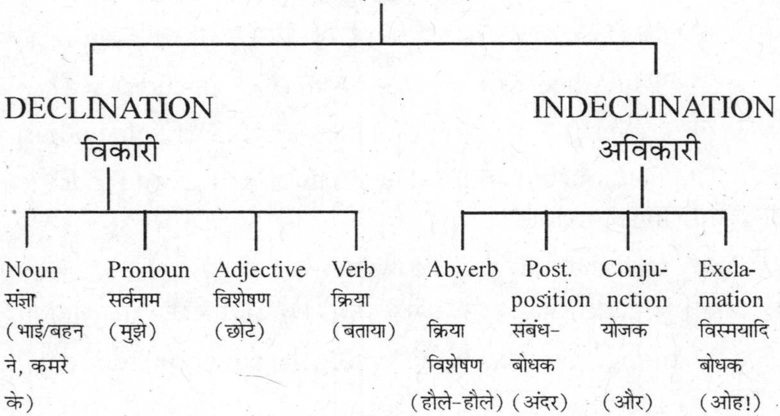

Noun संज्ञा

A **noun** is a word which is a name of anything.

There are three kinds of noun, in Hindi.

(i) व्यक्तिवाचक Proper noun

(ii) जातिवाचक Common noun

(iii) भाववाचक Abstract noun

गोपाल एक पुरुष है।	Gopal is a man.
मुम्बई एक नगर है।	Mumbai is a city.
बाइबिल एक पुस्तक है।	Bible is a book.

(i) गोपाल, मुम्बई and बाइबिल are the names of particular person, place and thing respectively. Thus these are **proper nouns.**

(ii) पुरुष, नगर and पुस्तक are the names of any person, place and thing of the same class respectively. Thus these are **common nouns.**

(iii) **Abstract noun** is the third kind of noun. It is a name of a quality, state or action, e.g., पुरुषत्व नागरिकता, ज्ञान etc.

Read out the following sentences—

(a) सच्चाई मनुष्य का सर्वोत्तम गुण है।	Truth is the best quality of man.
(b) मुझे अपने बचपन की याद है	I remember my childhood.
(c) मुस्कराहट में जीवन है।	The life lies in a smile.

In the above sentences सच्चाई, बचपन and मुस्कराहट are abstract nouns because these are the names of a quality, state or action respectively.

Abstract nouns are formed by three different ways:

(1) जातिवाचक संज्ञाओं से (from common nouns)

(2) विशेषणों से (from adjectives)

(3) क्रियाओं से (from verbs)

From common noun

Common nouns		Abstract nouns	Common nouns		Abstract nouns
शत्रु	–	शत्रुता; enmity	पुरुष	–	पुरुषत्व, manhood
मानव	–	मानवता; humanity	गुरु	–	गुरुत्व, eminence
मित्र	–	मित्रता; friendship	देव	–	देवत्व, godliness
लड़का	–	लड़कपन; boyhood	बच्चा	–	बचपन, childhood

From Adjectives

Adjectives		Abstract nouns	Adjectives		Abstract nouns
चतुर	–	चतुरता; cleverness	चतुर	–	चातुर्य, cleverness
सुंदर	–	सुंदरता; beauty	सुंदर	–	सौंदर्य, beauty
मधुर	–	मधुरता; sweetness	मधुर	–	माधुर्य, sweetness
लघु	–	लघुता; smallness	लघु	–	लघुत्व, smallness
बुरा	–	बुराई; evil	भला	–	भलाई, welfare
ऊँचा	–	ऊँचाई; highness	अच्छा	–	अच्छाई, goodness
चोर	–	चोरी; theft	सर्द	–	सर्दी, coldness
बूढ़ा	–	बुढ़ापा; old age	मोटा	–	मोटापा, fatness

From Verbs

Verbs		Abstract nouns	Verbs		Abstract nouns
समझना	–	समझ; knowledge	जाँचना	–	जाँच, investigation
झगड़ना	–	झगड़ा; dispute	छापना	–	छापा, printing
लड़ना	–	लड़ाई; battle	लिखना	–	लिखाई, writing
लिखना	–	लिखावट; writing	सजाना	–	सजावट, decoration
बचना	–	बचत; saving	खपना	–	खपत, consumption

REMARKABLE उल्लेखनीय

1. Here are some Hindi-suffixes which are attached to Nouns, Adjectives and Verbs for forming Abstract Noun respectively:
   (i) –ता, –त्व, –पन: Examples : मनुष्यता, देवत्व, बचपन
   (ii) –ता, –त्व, –आई, –ई, आपा –य Examples : सुंदरता, लघुत्व, नीचाई, गर्मी, बुढ़ापा, सौंदर्य
   (iii) –आई, आवट, आहट, –आ, त Examples : पढ़ाई, बनावट, घबराहट, झगड़ा, लिखत
2. Sometimes the roots itself become the Abstract Nouns—

Abstract noun	From the root infinitive
समझ	समझना
जाँच	जाँचना

8TH STEP आठवीं सीढ़ी

GENDER
लिंग

लिंग (Gender) is the distinction of sex. **Hindi** has only two genders— पुल्लिग (masculine), and स्त्रीलिंग (feminine).

(i) पुल्लिग – The names of males are always masculine.

(ii) स्त्रीलिंग– The names of females are always feminine,

Examples:

पुल्लिग Masculine	**स्त्रीलिंग feminine**
पुरुष (male), कुत्ता (dog)	स्त्री (female), कुतिया (bitch)
बैल (bull), सिंह (lion)	गाय (cow), सिंहनी (lioness)
ऊँट (camel), घोड़ा (horse)	ऊँटनी (she-camel), घोड़ी (mare)
लड़का (boy), नौकर (servant)	लड़की (girl), नौकरानी (maid-Servant)
धोबी (washerman), बूढ़ा (old-man)	धोबिन (washer-women), बुढ़िया (old woman)

रिश्ते Relations

पिता (father), पुत्र (son)	माता (mother), पुत्री (daughter)
भाई (brother), चाचा (uncle)	बहन (sister), चाची (aunt)
ताया/ताऊ (great uncle)	ताई (great aunt)
मामा (maternal uncle)	मामी (maternal aunt)
मौसा (husband of mother's sister)	मौसी (mother's sister)

फूफा (husband of father's sister)	फूफी (father's sister)
भांजा (nephew)	भांजी (niece)
भतीजा (brother's son)	भतीजी (brother's daughter)
दामाद (son-in-law)	बहू (daughter-in-law)
साला (brother-in-law wife's brother)	साली (sister-in-law, wife's sister)
देवर/जेठ (brother-in-law, husband's brother)	ननद (sister-in-law, husband's sister)
भाई	**बहन**
चचेरा cousin : son of uncle	चचेरी cousin : daughter of uncle
फुफेरा cousin : son of father's sister	फुफेरी cousin : daughter of father's sister
ममेरा cousin : son of mother's brother	ममेरी cousin : daughter of mother's brother
मौसंरा cousin : son of mother's sister	मौसेरी cousin : daughter of mother's sister

प्राणी-हीन पदार्थों का लिंग The Genders of Inanimate Objects

It is noticeable that Hindi has no neuter gender in it. That is why all inanimate objects and abstract nouns are either masculine or feminine. Thus, it is very difficult to differentiate the **actual gender of these objects.**

The genders of **inanimate** objects are to be settled by two means–

(i) अर्थ के आधार पर According to meaning.

(ii) रूप के आधार पर According to form.

1. Fixation of Gender–According to Meaning

पुल्लिग Masculine	**स्त्रीलिंग Feminine**
There are masculine–	These are feminine–
(1) Names of countries and	(1) Names of vans and

provinces, etc. भारत, पाकिस्तान, बांग्लादेश, जापान, बर्मा, अमरीका, इंग्लैंड, रूस, फ्रांस etc. पंजाब, हरियाणा, हिमाचल प्रदेश, उत्तर प्रदेश, तमिलनाडु, कर्नाटक, आंध्र प्रदेश, महाराष्ट्र, गुजरात, राजस्थान etc.

carriages etc. रेलगाड़ी, गाड़ी, बस, लारी, मोटर कार, नौका, नाव, किश्ती
Exceptions (अपवाद)– वायुयान, जलयान जहाज, **स्टीमर**, हवाई जहाज, ठेला, तांगा (**Mas**.)

(2) Names of hills and oceans, etc. हिमालय, विंध्याचल, सुमेरू पर्वत, हिंद महासागर, अंध महासागर, अरब सागर, लाल सागर
Exceptions– बंगाल की खाड़ी (Fem.)

(2) Names of rivers and canals– सतलुज, व्यास, रावी, चनाब, जेहलम, गंगा, यमुना, गोदावरी, कृष्णा, नर्मदा, ताप्ती
Exceptions– सिंधु, ब्रह्मपुत्र, सोन (Mas.)

(3) Names of division of time/months:
(i) क्षण, पल, सेकंड, मिनट, घंटा, सप्ताह, पक्ष, पखवाड़ा मास, महीना, वर्ष, साल आदि।
(ii) चैत्र, वैशाख, ज्येष्ठ, आषाढ़, श्रावण, कार्तिक, पौष, माघ, भाद्रपद, फाल्गुन आदि (देसी माह), और जनवरी, फरवरी, मार्च, अप्रैल, आदि (अंग्रेजी माह)
(iii) सोमवार, मंगलवार, बुधवार etc.

(3) Names of तिथियाँ (lunar days): प्रथमा, द्वितीया, पंचमी, अष्टमी, दशमी, द्वादशी, अमावस्या, पूर्णिमा, दूज, तीज, चौदस, आदि।

(4) Names of planets: सूर्य, चंद्र, मंगल, बुध, शनि, राहु, केतु etc.
Exeption– पृथ्वी **(Fem.)**

(4) Names of spices: इलायची, सुपारी, मिर्च, दालचीनी, हल्दी, मुलहठी
Exceptions– नमक, जीरा, अदरक

(5) Names of metals:
सोना, लोहा, कांसा, तांबा, टीन, etc.
Exception– चाँदी **(Fem.)**

(6) Names of jewels:
हीरा, पन्ना, पुखराज, नीलम, मोती etc.
Exception– मणि **(Fem.)**

(7) Names of trees:
पीपल, आम, बड़ etc.
तरकारी, सब्जी, खिचड़ी etc.

(5) Names of stars:
अश्विनी, भरणी, मृगशिरा, स्वाती, etc.

(6) Names of languages:
हिंदी, पंजाबी, उर्दू, बंगला, मलयालम, कन्नड, तेलुगु, मराठी, गुजराती, सिंधी, etc.

(7) Names of food-stuffs:
पूरी, कचौड़ी, रोटी, दाल, भाजी,
Exception– परांठा, दलिया **(Mas.)**

2. Fixation of Gender–According to Form

पुल्लिग Masculine

(1) Hindi words ending–
–आ, –आव, –पन & –पा:
पैसा, कपड़ा, लोटा, छाता, बहाव, फैलाव, चढ़ाव, बचपन, लड़कपन, बुढ़ापा, etc.

(2) Sanskrit nouns ending in–त्व, –य, –त & –न
पशुत्व, महत्व, सत्त्व, हिंदुत्व, सौंदर्य, कार्य, माधुर्य, चरित्र, गीत, पतन, पालन, शासन, etc.

स्त्रीलिंग Feminine

(1) Hindi words ending–
–आई, –या, –वट & –हट:
सफाई, पढ़ाई, लिखाई, ऊँचाई, चिड़िया, बिटिया, खटिया, बनावट, लिखावट, सजावट, घबराहट, चिकनाहट, etc.

(2) Sanskrit nouns ending in–ता, –आ, –इ & –ई
पशुता, महत्ता, सत्ता, आवश्यकता, माला, शोभा, दया, इच्छा, मति, बुद्धि, वृद्धि, हानि, नदी, सखी, धरती, etc.

Actually, the gender-system, in Hindi, is extremely arbitrary. Of course, there are certain rules by which the gender of most of the nouns may be determined. But that is not final at all. There are many exceptions. The non-Hindi-speaking learners should keep this fact in mind. There is no need of being nervous. The learner should take help from dictionaries and listen correct Hindi speeches.

Try in the right direction and you will find that you are on progress.

REMARKABLE उल्लेखनीय

1. The English word 'cousin' stands for all these—

   (i) ममेरा। फुफेरा। मौसेरा। चचेरा भाई।

   (ii) ममेरी। फुफेरी। मौसेरी। चचेरी बहन।

   In hindi, all these words are used for the particular relations.

2. The English word 'uncle' stands for all these—

   मामा। फूफा। मौसा। चाचा

   Thus 'aunt' stands for—

   मामी। फुफी। मौसी। चाची।

   In Hindi, these words are separately used for the said relations.

3. The word 'uncle' is used for the father's brother, whether he may be elder or younger. But in Hindi, there are separate words: ताया for father's elder brother and चाचा for father's younger brother.

9TH STEP नौवीं सीढ़ी

NUMBER
वचन

Like English and many other Indian regional languages, there are two numbers in Hindi— (i) एकवचन (Singular) and (ii) बहुवचन (Plural). Hindi does not recognize the द्विवचन (dual number) found in **Sanskrit**. All nouns, pronouns and verbs fall under these two heads of number.

All the nouns change their forms according to their numbers and genders.

When we are discussing separately number, we shall treat masculine and feminine nouns separately. **Look at the following words. You will see that they are categorically set.**

(i) Masculine	*(ii) Feminine*
फल (fruit) अ– ending word	आँख (eye) अ– ending word
राजा (king) आ– ending word	माता (mother) आ– ending word
मुनि (sage) इ– ending word	तिथि (date) इ– ending word
सुधी (wise man) ई– ending word	नदी (river) ई– ending word
साधु (saint) उ– ending word	वस्तु (thing) उ– ending word
	बहू (daughter-in-law) ऊ– ending word
	गौ (cow) औ– ending word

(i) फल, राज़ा, मुनि, सुधी & साधु are masculine nouns.

(ii) आँख, माता, तिथि, नदी, वस्तु, बहू & गौ are feminine nouns.

फल & आँख are अ– ending words, राजा & माता are आ– ending words. They are alike in vowels-endings. But it is noticeable that forms of फल and आँख, राजा and माता, मुनि and तिथि, etc. will be unlike.

The plural forms of masculine and feminine nouns go separately according to their own rules. You will learn it in the following chart.

Masculine noun

Singular	*Plural*	*Oblique singular*	*Oblique plural*
फल	फल	फल ने	फलों ने
राजा	राजा	राजा ने	राजाओं ने
मुनि	मुनि	मुनि ने	मुनियों ने
सुधी	सुधी	सुधी ने	सुधियों ने
साधु	साधु	साधु ने	साधुओं ने

Feminine noun

Singular	*Plural*	*Oblique singular*	*Oblique plural*
आँख	आँखें	आँख ने	आँखों ने
माता	माताएँ	माता ने	माताओं ने
तिथि	तिथियाँ	तिथि ने	तिथियों ने
नदी	नदियाँ	नदी ने	नदियों ने
वस्तु	वस्तुएँ	वस्तु ने	वस्तुओं ने
बहू	बहुएँ	बहू ने	बहुओं ने
गौ	गौएँ	गौ ने	गौओं ने

Thus in numbers, feminine nouns can be differentiated from masculine nouns.

There are both the forms (singular and plural) of the nouns in both the genders, in the following:

Masculine		*Feminine*	
(अ)		(-अ)	
Singular	*Plural*	*Singular*	*Plural*
दिन (day)	दिन (days)	रात (night)	रातें (nights)
नारियल (coconut)	नारियल (coconuts)	तलवार (sword)	तलवारें (swords)
कागज (paper)	कागज (papers)	किताब (book)	किताबें (books)
काम (work)	काम (works)	बहन (sister)	बहनें (sisters)
आम (mango)	आम(mangoes)	भूल (error)	भूलें (errors)
घर (house)	घर (houses)	बात (matter)	बातें (matters)
(-आ)		(-आ)	
बच्चा (child)	बच्चे(children)	कक्षा (class)	कक्षाएँ (classes)
पत्ता (leaf)	पत्ते (leaves)	आज्ञा (order)	आज्ञाएँ (orders)
कपड़ा (cloth)	कपड़े (clothes)	हवा (wind)	हवाएँ (winds)
कमरा (room)	कमरे (rooms)	संख्या (number)	संख्याएँ (numbers)
कौआ (crow)	कौए (crows)	चिड़िया (bird)	चिड़ियों (birds)
मामा (mother's brother)	मामा (mother's brothers)	चाची (aunt)	चाचियाँ (aunts)
Singular	***Plural***	***Singular***	***Plural***
पति (husband)	पति (husbands)	पंक्ति (row)	पंक्तियाँ (rows)
आदमी (man)	आदमी (men)	पत्नी (wife)	पत्नियाँ (wives)
हाथी (elephant)	हाथी (elephants)	लड़की (girl)	लड़कियाँ (girls)
साथी (fellow)	साथी (fellows)	बच्ची (female-child)	बच्चियाँ (female-children)
भाई (brother)	भाई (brothers)	लकड़ी (wood)	लकड़ियाँ (woods)
नाई (hair-dresser)	नाई (hair-dressers)	खिड़की (window)	खिड़कियाँ (windows)

पानी (water)	पानी (waters)	चिट्ठी (letter)	चिट्ठियाँ (letters)
साधु (saint)	साधु (saints)	बुढ़िया (old-woman)	बुढ़िया (old-women)
डाकू (dacoit)	डाकू (dacoits)	वधू (daugther-in-law)	वधुएँ (daughers-in-law)

REMARKABLE उल्लेखनीय

1. Some Sanskrit Masculine nouns ending in –आ do not change in plural–

Singular	Plural
नेता (leader)	नेता (leaders)
श्रोता (listner)	श्रोता (listners)
वक्ता (speaker)	वक्ता(speakers)
मंत्री (minister)	मंत्री (ministers)

But usually 'गण' (group) is added in the singular to make plural. It is noticeable that गण indicates many persons in number. Example: नेतागण, श्रोतागण etc.

This rule applies in पाठकगण, दर्शकगण, छात्रगण, मुनिगण also.

2. प्राण, दर्शन, आँसू, केश are always applied in the plural form. हमारे प्राण, आपके दर्शन, दुखियों के आँसू, नारियों के केश, etc.

10TH STEP दसवीं सीढ़ी

CASE & DECLENTION OF NOUNS
कारक एवं संज्ञा-शब्दों के रूप

Case कारक

There are eight cases in Hindi expressed by different post-positions or case-endings. The post-positions mostly correspond to English prepositions. The post-positions (विभक्तियाँ) of all the cases are as given below:

	Case	Post-positions	Usage
1.	कर्त्ता Nominative	X, ने	राम, राम ने
2.	कर्म Objective	को, to	राम को
3.	कारण Instrumental	से, के द्वारा with, by	राम से, राम के द्वारा
4.	सम्प्रदान Dative	को, के लिए for	राम को, राम के लिए
5.	अपादान Ablative	से (जुदाई-departure) from, for, since, than	राम से
6.	संबंध Possessive	का, के, की of, 's	राम का, राम के, राम की
7.	अधिकरण Locative	में, पर, से ऊपर, के ऊपर in, at, on, above, upon	राम में, राम पर, राम से ऊपर, राम के ऊपर

8. संबोधन अरे, अरी, हे, री हे राम!
Vocative

Learn the usage of cases in the following pharases or sentences. All the cases have been given respectively.

1. कर्ता कारक

(i) राम आया।	Ram came.
(ii) राम ने कहा।	Ram said.

It is worth remembering that the case-ending or post-position ने is used mostly after the nominatives of transitive verbs in the past tense.

2. कर्म कारक

(i) इस पुस्तक को ले जाओ।	Take this book
(ii) राम को **मेहनत** करनी चाहिए।	Ram should work hard.

3. करण कारक

(i) अपने हाथ से यहां दस्तखत कीजिए।	Please sign here with your hand.
(ii) यह अमित के द्वारा लिखा	**It is written by Amit.** गया है।

4. संप्रदान कारक

(i) आभा को यह पुस्तक दो।	**Give this book** to Abha
(ii) मां के लिए एक कप दूध लाओ।	Bring a cup of milk for mother.

5. कर्म कारक

(i) पेड़ से पत्ता गिरता है।	Leaf falls from the tree.
(ii) मैं आश्रम से आ रहा हूँ।	I am coming from the Ashram.

6. अपादान कारक

(i) विकास राखी का भाई है।	Vikas is the brother of Rakhi.
(ii) मैं आगरा के किले में गया।	I went to the fort to Agra.

(iii) लक्ष्मी बाई झांसी की रानी थीं।	Luxmi Bai was the queen of Jhansi.

7. अधिकरण कारक

(i) हम कमरे में बैठे हैं।	We are sitting in the room.
(ii) मेज पर पुस्तक पड़ी है।	The book is on the table.

8. संबोधन कारक

(i) हे भगवान! मेरी रक्षा करो।	O God! Save me.
(ii) ऐ बच्चो! भाग जाओ।	O children! Run away.
(iii) अरी लड़की! इधर आ।	O girl! Come here.

Declension of nouns संज्ञाशब्दों की रूपावली

The mode of declension of a noun depends on its ending and gender. In Hindi all nouns ends in vowels. Two examples of declension of nouns are given below:

पुल्लिग शब्द 'लड़का' Boy (आकारांत)

(Masculine ending in आ)

Case	*Singular*	*Plural*
1. Nom.	लड़का/लड़के ने	लड़का/लड़कों ने
2. Obj.	लड़के को	लड़कों को
3. Ins.	लड़के से/के द्वारा	लड़कों से/के द्वारा
4. Dat.	लड़के को/के लिए	लड़कों को/के लिए
5. Abl.	लड़के से	लड़कों से
6. Poss.	लड़के का/के/की	लड़कों का/के/की
7. Loc.	लड़के में/पर	लड़कों में/पर
8. Vec.	ऐ लड़के!	ऐ लड़कों!

All such masculine nouns ending in आ are declined like लड़का, घोड़ा, कमरा, चमड़ा, बछड़ा, बच्चा, गमला।

कुछ अन्य संज्ञाओं की सांकेतिक रूपावली Indicative declension of some more nouns.

Two cases are to be **distinguished**–(i) Direct and (ii) Oblique. The direct case remains without **post-position**. On the contrary, oblique occurs mostly with the post-positions.

1. Masculine 'बालक' शब्द अ–ending : एकवचन Singular

सीधा Direct: Nominative cases	:	बालक
तिर्यक Oblique: All the cases	:	बालक ने/को/से/के लिए/से/का/में/हे/बालक!
		बहुवचन Plural
सीधा Direct: Nominative cases	:	बालकों
तिर्यक Oblique: All the cases	:	बालकों ने/को/से/के लिए/से/का/में/ हे बालको!

2. Masculine इ– ending, ई– ending, उ– ending, ऊ– ending:

	Singular	***Plural wihout post-position***	***Plural with post-position***
इ– ending	मुनि	मुनि	मुनियों ने/को/से etc.
ई– ending	हाथी	हाथी	हाथियों ने/को/से etc.
उ– ending	साधु	साधु	साधुओं ने/को/से etc.
ऊ– ending	डाकू	डाकू	डाकुओं ने/को/से etc.

आ– ending words (i) चाचा etc., showing relationship, and (ii) loan words राजा etc., from Sanskrit are declined differently as under–

(i)	चाचा	चाचा	चाचाओं ने/को/से etc.
(ii)	राजा	राजा	राजाओं ने/को/से etc.
(i)	मामा	मामा	मामाओं ने/को/से etc.
(ii)	देवता	देवता	देवताओं ने/को/से etc.

स्त्रीलिंग शब्द 'लड़की' Girl (ईकारांत)

(Feminine ending in ई)

Case	*Singular*	*Plural*
1.	लड़की/लड़की ने	लड़कियां/लड़कियों ने
2.	लड़की को	लड़कियों को
3.	लड़की से/के द्वारा	लड़कियों से/के द्वारा
4.	लड़की को/के लिए	लड़कियों को/के लिए
5.	लड़की से	लड़कियों से
6.	लड़की का/के/की	लड़कियों का/के/की
7.	लड़की में/पर	लड़कियों में/पर
8.	हे लड़की!	हे लड़कियों!

Most of the feminine nouns ending in ई are declined like लड़की।
Some nouns are: श्रीमती, नदी, रोटी, धोती, नारी।

Feminine अ, आ, इ, ई, उ, ऊ, औ– ending nouns:

	Singular	*Plural wihout post-position*	*Plural with post-position*
अ– ending	रात	रातें	रातों ने/को/से etc.
आ– ending	छात्रा	छात्राएँ	छात्राओं की/पर etc.
इ– ending	जाति	जातियाँ	जातियों ने/की etc.
ई– ending	कहानी	कहानियाँ	कहानियों के लिए/में etc.
उ– ending	वस्तु	वस्तुएँ	वस्तुओं को/से etc.
ऊ– ending	बहू	बहुएँ	बहुओं से/पर/के लिए /अरी बहुओ! etc.
औ– ending	गौ	गौएँ	गौओं ने/को/से/री गौओ! etc.
इया– ending	चिड़िया	चिड़ियाँ	चिड़ियों ने/के लिए/हे चिड़ियों! etc.

REMARKABLE उल्लेखनीय

1. In English, there are prepositions but in Hindi, there are post-positions. The clause 'on the road' is translated into Hindi 'सड़क पर'– that is why 'on' is preposition (because it comes before the noun) but 'पर' is postposition (because it follows the noun).
2. There are two forms of case (i) direct and (ii) oblique.

Masculine:	Direct:	लड़का	लड़के
	Oblique:	लड़के ने	लड़कों ने
Feminine:	Direct:	नदी	नदियां
	Oblique:	नदी ने	नदियों ने etc.

3. ने is attched to the subject of a Transitive Verb when it is used in the past tense.

PART 2
WORD

11TH STEP ग्यारहवीं सीढ़ी

PRONOUN
सर्वनाम

सर्वनाम (Pronoun) is a word used in place of noun. Actually it represents, a noun. In Hindi, there are six kinds of pronoun–

(1)	पुरुषवाचक Personal	: मैं (I), तुम (you), वह (he/she/it), आप (you आदरसूचक honorific)
(2)	निश्चयवाचक Definite	: यह (this), वह (that)
(3)	अनिश्चयवाचक Indefinite	: कोई (somebody), कुछ (some)
(4)	प्रश्नवाचक Interrogative	: कौन (who), क्या (what)
(5)	संबंधवाचक Relative	: जो (who, which)
(6)	निजवाचक Reflexive	: स्वयं (self) for all persons

Pronouns have no संबोधन कारक (Vocative case)

There are three पुरुष in Hindi grammer:

(i) उत्तम पुरुष First person —मैं, हम

(ii) मध्यम पुरुष Second person —तुम, आप (आदरसूचक)

(iii) अन्य पुरुष Third person —वह, वे

सर्वनाम शब्दों की रूपावली Declension of Pronouns

मैं *(I) First Person.*

(i) मैं/मैंने- हम/हमने (v) मुझसे-हमसे

(ii)	मुझको/मुझे–हमको/हमें	(vi)	मेरा/मेरे/मेरी–हमारा/हमारे/हमारी
(iii)	मुझसे–हमसे	(vii)	मुझमें/मुझ पर–हममें/हम पर
(iv)	मुझको/मेरे लिए– हमको/हमारे लिए		

तू *(Thou) Second Person*

(i)	तू/तूने– तुम/तुमने	(v)	तुझसे–तुमसे
(ii)	तुझको–तुमको	(vi)	तेरा/तेरे/तेरी–तुम्हारा/ तुम्हारे/तुम्हारी
(iii)	तुझसे/तुम्हारे द्वारा–तुमसे/ तुम्हारे द्वारा	(vii)	तुझमें/तुझ पर–तुममें/तुम पर
(iv)	तुझको/तुम्हारे लिए– तुमको/तुम्हारे लिए		

वह *(He/She/It) Third Person*

(i)	वह/उसने– वे/उन्होंने	(v)	उससे–उनसे
(ii)	उसको/उसे–उनको/ उन्हें	(vi)	उसका/उसके/उसकी–उनका/ उनके/उनकी
(iii)	उससे/उसके द्वारा– उनसे/उनके द्वारा	(vii)	उसमें/उस पर–उनमें/उन पर
(iv)	उसको/उसके लिए– उनको/उनके लिए		

आप आदरसूचक (You-honorific) Second Person

एकवचन— 1. आप/आपने, 2. आपको, 3. आपसे, 4. के लिए (को), 5. से, 6. का/के/की, 7. में (पर)

बहुवचन— 1. आप लोगों का/आप लोगों ने, 2. आप लोगों को, 3. आप लोगों से, 4. आप लोगों को/आप लोगों के लिए, 5. आप लोगों से, 6. आप लोगों का/के/की, 7. आप लोगों में/आप लोगों पर।

Let us use some pronouns into the sentences:

1. मैं इस बारे में कुछ नहीं जानता। I do not know anything about it.
2. हम वहां नहीं जाना चाहते। We do not want to go there.
3. वह अब क्या करेगा? What will he do now?
4. यह बिल्कुल ठीक है। It is quite right.
5. आप पूना में कहाँ ठहरेंगे? Where will you stay at Pune?
6. मैं आप वहीं उपस्थित था। I myself was present there.
7. कोई आने वाला है। Someone has to come.
8. ऐसा कौन कहता है? Who says it?
9. अब आपको क्या चाहिए? What do you want now?
10. कुछ फल खा लो। Take some fruit.

REMARKABLE उल्लेखनीय

The pronouns आप ap, तुम tum and तू tu have different honorific values.

आप is used in addressing one's seniors. It is used with a third person plural verb whether the reference is to one person or more than one. तुम tum is used in addressing one's relatives or close friends. It is also used to address persons of lower status than the speaker.

तू tu expresses the feelings of contempt and insignficance. It is also used in addressing God.

12TH STEP ग्यारहवीं सीढ़ी

ADJECTIVE
विशेषण

विशेषण (Adjective) is a word used to qualify a noun or a pronoun. Adjectives in Hindi has four kinds—

(1)	गुणवाचक	Qualitative
(2)	संख्यावाचक	Numeral
(3)	परिमाणवाचक	Quantitative
(4)	सार्वनामिक	Pronominal or Demonstrative

Let us use adjectives into sentences—

(i)	गौरव अच्छा लड़का है।	Gaurav is a good boy.
(ii)	वेद चार हैं।	There are four Vedas.
(iii)	पांच लीटर दूध लाओ।	Bring five litres of milk
(iv)	यह पुस्तक मेरी है।	This book is mine.

'अच्छा लड़का', 'चार वेद', 'पांच लीटर दूध' and 'यह पुस्तक'–in these phrases। अच्छा, चार, पांच and यह are गुणवाचक, संख्यावाचक, परिमाणवाचक and सार्वनामिक विशेषण respectively.

Hindi adjectives fall under two heads— (i) Inflected, and (ii) Un-inflected.

(i) आ–ending adjectives are inflected. आ of singular masculine changes into ए for plural masculine. आ changes into ई for feminine singular and plural. Examples:

Singular	अच्छा बच्चा	अच्छे बच्चे
Plural	अच्छी बच्ची	अच्छी बच्चियाँ

(ii) Adjectives which end in other vowels than आ are uninflected. They do not change. Examples:

Singular	सुंदर बालक	सुंदर बालक
Plural	सुंदर बालिका	सुंदर बालिकाएँ

विशेषण की तुलनावस्था Comparison in Adjectives

1. सोनिया लम्बी है।
2. आभा सोनिया से लम्बी है।
3. मीनाक्षी सबसे लम्बी है।

We see in the above sentences, three degrees of adjective लम्बी। Hindi adjectives do not have any separate form to show the degrees of comparsion. But some adjectives have different forms of Sanskrit degrees, such as:

Positive	***Comparative***	***Superlative***
उच्च	उच्चतर	उच्चतम
निम्न	निम्नतर	निम्नतम
सरल	सरलतर	सरलतम
लघु	लघुतर	लघुतम
अधिक	अधिकतर	अधिकतम
दीर्घ	दीर्घतर	दीर्घतम
श्रेष्ठ	श्रेष्ठतर	श्रेष्ठतम
निकट	निकटतर	निकटतम
प्रिय	प्रियतर	प्रियतम
नवीन	नवीनतर	नवीनतम

Some adjectives are given in the following columns—

Qualitative	***Numeral***	***Quantitative***	***Pronominal***
नया	दस	दस (किलो)	यह (पेन)

(New)	(Ten)	Ten (kilo)	This (Pen)
दैनिक	आधा	सारा (धन)	वह (गौ)
(Daily)	(Half)	All (Money)	That (Cow)
सुंदर	चौथा	कुछ (दूध)	जो (कुत्ता)
(Beautiful)	(Fourth)	Some (Milk)	Which (Dog)
स्वस्थ	दुगुना	दो (मीटर)	वो (पुस्तक)
(Healthy)	(Double)	Two (Metre)	That (Book)
काला	अकेला	और (घी)	कौन (बालक)
(Black)	(Alone)	More (Ghee)	Which (Boy)
अच्छा	कुछ	सारा (पानी)	उस (घर में)
(Good)	(Some)	Whole (Water)	In that (House)

विशेषणों की रचना Formation of Adjectives (From Nouns)

(i) By adding– शाली to Sanskrit Nouns—

बल	बलशाली	प्रतिभा	प्रतिभाशाली
शक्ति	शक्तिशाली	भाग्य	भाग्यशाली

(ii) By adding– वान or मान to Sanskrit Nouns—

धन	धनवान	गुण	गुणवान
श्री	श्रीमान	बुद्धि	बुद्धिमान

(iii) By adding– इक to Sanskrit Nouns—

राजनीति	राजनैतिक	नीति	नैतिक
मास	मासिक	उद्योग	औद्योगिक
इतिहास	ऐतिहासिक	भूगोल	भौगोलिक
दिन	दैनिक	सेना	सैनिक

(iv) By adding– इत to Sanskrit Nouns—

संबंध	संबंधित	आनंद	आनंदित
सम्मान	सम्मानित	शिक्षा	शिक्षित

(v) By adding– ईय to Sanskrit Nouns—

पर्वत	पर्वतीय	राष्ट्र	राष्ट्रीय
भारत	भारतीय	विभाग	विभागीय

(vi) By adding– ई

जंगल	जंगली	सुख	सुखी
संन्यास	संन्यासी	देस	देसी
परदेस	परदेसी	लोभ	लोभी

(v) By adding– ईला to Sanskrit Nouns—

चमक	चमकीला	रौब	रौबीला
भड़क	भड़कीला	जोश	जोशीला

REMARKABLE उल्लेखनीय

1. (i) Usually– सा is added to quantitative adjectives— to intensify the meaning; as — बहुत–सा a great deal, थोड़ा–सा a little.

(ii) Sometimes— सा is used to denote the lesser degree of the quality, as— नन्हीं–सी गुड़िया a little doll, थोड़ी–सी जगह a small space.

(iii) –सा either denotes looking or similar—

(a) looking—

काला–सा black-looking	पीला–सा pale-looking
मोटा–सा fat-looking	पतला–सा thin-looking

(b) similar—

एक–सा similar	तुम–सा like you
उस–सा (mas.) like him	मुझ–सा like me
उस–सा (fem.) like her	हम–सा like us

13TH STEP तेरहवीं सीढ़ी

VERB
क्रिया

क्रिया (Verb) is a word which tells us something about a person, place or thing.

Verbs are generally of two kinds— (i) Transitive and (ii) Intransitive.

(i) सकर्मक क्रिया Transitive Verb (A word which requires the object). as—मीनाक्षी कार्य करती है। Here करती है is a transitive verb, because it requires the object कार्य to complete its sense.

(ii) अकर्मक क्रिया Intransitive Verb (A word which has no object. It completes the sense itself). as— पूजा चलती है। Here चलती है is an intransitive verb because it has no object.

Here are some transitive verbs and intransitive verbs. These should be noticed.

1. सकर्मक क्रिया Transitive Verbs

करना	to do	सुनना	to hear
पढ़ना	to read	कहना	to tell
लिखना	to write	रखना	to keep
देखना	to see	लेना	to take
जानना	to know	देना	to give

2. अकर्मक क्रिया Intransitive Verbs

चलना	do walk	आना	to come
रहना	to live	जाना	to go

उठना	to rise	होना	to be
सोना	to sleep	गिरना	to fall
हँसना	to laugh	पहुँचना	to reach

Both the verbs, transtive and intransitive, has two basic parts

(i) सामान्य क्रिया The Infinitive

(ii) धातु The Root

(i) सामान्य क्रिया is the original form of a verb always ending in 'ना', as 'पढ़ना' (go read), रखना (to put), चलना (to walk), etc.

(ii) धातु is obtained by cutting off the ना from the infinitive as (read), 'रख' (put), 'चल' (walk), etc.

Actually all the verbs take their forms from धातु– the root. In other words, the root is basic verb and the addition of 'ना' gives it its सामान्य रूप – the infinitive form.

Let us learn some infinitive verbs (transitive and intransitive verbs) and practise their roots.

Transitive Verbs

Infinitives		*Roots*	*Infinitives*		*Roots*
खरीदना	to buy	खरीद	खाना	to eat	खा
बेचना	to sell	बेच	पीना	to drink	पी
समझना	to understand	समझ	बोलना	to speak	बोल
धोना	to wash	धो	पकड़ना	to catch	पकड़
गाना	to sing	गा	तोड़ना	to break	तोड़

Intransitive Verbs

Infinitives		**Roots**	**Infinitives**		**Roots**
ठहरना	to stay	ठहर	दिखना	to appear	दिख
डरना	to fear	डर	हँसना	to laugh	हँस
रोना	to weep	रो	खेलना	to play	खेल
मरना	to die	मर	लड़ना	to quarrel	लड़
निकलना	to come out	निकल	होना	to be	हो

विधि रूप Imperative Mood

The imperative mood is used when we command, advice or request any person to do a thing.

Look at the following sentences carefully—

(1)	निबंध लिखो।	Write an essay.
	यहां बैठ।	sit here.
	चाय ला।	Bring tea.
	उसे बुला।	Call him.
	पुस्तक पढ़।	Read the book
(2)	दूध लाओ।	Bring milk.
	शांत रहो।	Keep quite.
	गीत गाओ	Sing a song.
	खिड़की खोलो।	Open the window.
	काम करो।	Do the work.
(3)	कृपया आइए।	Please come.
	कृपया घर पर रहिए।	Stay at home please.
	कृपया बाहर जाइए।	Please go out.

Watch the sentences of group (1), (2) and (3). You will find some difference among them. One thing is common in these sentences, i.e. the subject– तू, तुम and आप are omitted respectively.

(i) तू is generally used to address servants. It is not used for addressing equals. Examples.

रामू (तू) दो कप चाय ला।	Ramu, (thou) bring two cups of tea.

(ii) तुम is used while we address friends, equals or youngers. Examples:

भाई, तुम आज विद्यालय क्यों नहीं गए?	Brother, why did you not go to the school today?
देवेन्द्र, मेरे घर अवश्य आना।	Devendra, do come to my house.

(iii) आप is used for addressing superiors and persons whom we wish to respect. Examples:

मामा जी, आप मेरे साथ आइए।	Uncle, come with me, please.
श्रीमान्, कृपया आप मेरी बात सुनिए।	Sir, you listen to me, please.

मत may be used to express the meaning of negative. It may be used before or after a verb. Examples:

मत हँसो।	Don't laugh.
रोओ मत।	Don't weep.
शोर मत करो।	Don't make a noise.
वहां मत बैठिए।	Don't sit there, please.

REMARKABLE उल्लेखनीय

1. धातु or Root of the verb is ascertained by removing 'ना' of the infinitive verb—i.e., root is खा of infinitive verb खाना, पी of infinitive verb पीना.
2. Imperative sentences in Hindi, are formed in two ways—
   (a) in ordinary way, and
   (b) in honorific way.
   (a) Again in ordinary way, the imperative sentences are formed
      (i) by using the root धातु of the verb खा, पढ़, लिख etc. and
      (ii) by adding ओ vowel or its sign to the root of the verb, as खाओ, पढ़ो, लिखो etc.
   (b) Honorific imperatives are formed by adding ए or इ, ए vowel or its sign to the root of the verb, as— खाएं, पढ़ें, लिखें as well as खाइए, पढ़िए, लिखिए etc.

14TH STEP चौदहवीं सीढ़ी

TENSE (1)
काल (1)

काल (Tense) of a verb shows the time of an action. There are three main tenses in Hindi:

(i)	वर्तमान काल	Present Tense
(ii)	भविष्यत् काल	Future Tense
(iii)	भूत काल	Past Tense

We shall study all the three tenses respectively.

वर्तमान काल Present Tense

The Present tense may be divided into three kinds:

(1)	सामान्य वर्तमान	Present Indefinite
(2)	तात्कालिक वर्तमान	Present Continuous
(3)	सम्भाव्य वर्तमान	Doubtful Present

1. सामान्य वर्तमान Present Indefinite

Here is the conjugation of हो (be) in the present tense.

	Masculine	*Translation*	*Feminine*
Ist Person:	मैं हूँ।	I am	मैं हूँ।
	तू है।		तुम हो।
IIst Person:	तुम हो।	You are	आप हैं। (in respect)

IIIrd Person:	वह है।	He is, She is	वह है।
	वे हैं।	They are	वे हैं।

हो is a helping verb. It helps the main verb.

The following is the conjugation of main verb पढ़ (read) in the present indefinite. –ता –ते–ती (the suffixes) are added to the root.

Ist Person:	मैं पढ़ता/पढ़ती हूँ।	I read
	हम पढ़ते/पढ़ती हैं।	We read
IInd Person:	तू पढ़ता/पढ़ती है।	You read
	तुम पढ़ते/पढ़ती हो।	You read
IIIrd Person:	वह पढ़ता/पढ़ती है।	He/She reads
	वे पढ़ते/पढ़ती हैं।	They read

Other verbs are also conjugated in the same way.

When we wish to form a negative sentence in present indefinite, we put नहीं before the main verb, and omit हूँ, हो or हैं। Examples:

हम नहीं पढ़ते।	We do not read.
तू नहीं पढ़ता।	You do not read
वे नहीं पढ़ते।	They do not read.

2. तात्कालिक् वर्तमान Present Continuous—

(रहा, रहे, रही are added to the root following the form हो accordingly)

Ist Person:	मैं खा रहा/रही हूँ।	I am eating.
	हम खा रहे/रही हैं।	We are eating.
IInd Person:	तू खा रहा/रही है।	You are eating.
	तुम खा रहे/रही हो।	You are eating.
IIIrd Person:	वह खा रहा/रही है।	He/She is eating.
	वे खा रहे/रही हैं।	They are eating.

In feminine gender रहा and रहे are changed into रही

3. संभाव्य वर्तमान Doubtful Present—

[–ता, –ते, –ती are added to the root following the form हो (हूँगा/होंगे/होगा etc., in masculine, and हूँगी/होंगी/होगी etc., in feminine)].

	Masculine	English	Feminine
Ist Person—			
Singular:	मैं जाता हूँगा।	I may be going	मैं जाती हूँगी।
Plural:	हम जाते होंगे।	We may be going	हम जाती होंगी।
IInd Person—			
Singular:	तू जाता होगा।	You may be going	तू जाती होगी।
Plural:	तुम जाते होगे।	We may be going	तुम जाती होगी।
IIIrd Person—			
Singular:	वह जाता होगा।	He may be going	
		She may be going	वह जाती होगी।
Plural:	वे जाते होंगे।	They may be going	वे जाती होंगी।

In the feminine gender –ता, –ते are changed into –ती and –गा–गे are changed into –गी।

भविष्यत् काल Future Tense

The future tense may be classified into two kinds

(1) सामान्य भविष्यत् — Future Indefinite.

(2) सम्भाव्य भविष्यत् — Doubtful Future

1. सामान्य भविष्यत् Future Indefinite—

(–ऊँगा, –ओगे, –एगा, –एँगे etc., are added to the root of the verb in masculines) and –ऊँगी, –ओगी, –एगी, –एँगी etc., in feminines.

Here is the conjugation of देख in the Future Indefinite.

Ist —	मैं देखूँगा/देखूँगी।	I shall see.
	हम देखेंगे/देखेगी।	We shall see.
IInd —	तू देखेगा/देखेगी।	You will see.
	तुम देखोगे/देखोगी।	You will see.

IIIrd —	वह देखेगा/देखेंगी।	He/She will see.
	वे देखेंगे/देखेगी।	They will see.

2. संभाव्य भविष्यत् Contingent Future—

[This tense is formed by adding –ऊँ, –ए, –एँ–ओ, to the root according to person and number.]

Following is the conjugation of खेल in the Contingent Future—

Ist —	मैं खेलूँ।	I may play.
	हम खेलें।	We may play.
IInd —	तू खेल।	You may play.
	तुम खेलो।	You may play.
IIIrd —	वह खेले।	He may play.
	वे खेलें।	They may play.

Contingent Future expresses भविष्य में संभावना (possibility in Future), इच्छा (willingness), सुझाव (suggestion), उद्देश्य (purpose), शर्त (condition), etc. Examples:

(i) भविष्यं में सम्भावना, हो न हो,
कहीं वह आ न जाए। — Lest he may come.

(ii) भविष्य में इच्छा
अनु से कहो कि किताबें लाए। — Ask Anu to bring the books.

(iii) भविष्य में सुझाव–
ऐसा क्यों न करें? — Why not do this?

(iv) भविष्य में उद्देश्य–
तुम एक वैज्ञानिक बनो। — You become a scientist.

(v) भविष्य में शर्त–
यदि वे आएँ तो तुम भी आ जाना। — It they come, you do come.

REMARKABLE उल्लेखनीय

I have just finished it मैंने इसे अभी समाप्त किया है।

In English, the above sentence is in present perfect. But in Hindi, it is not in present tense. It is called in आसन्न भूत (which can be found in 15th step)

'I have just finished it' can be expressed in two ways in Hindi—

(i) मैंने इसे अभी समाप्त किया है।

(ii) मैं इसे अभी समाप्त कर चुका हूँ।

As you know, आसन्न भूत is formed by addding है in the singular and हैं in the plural, to the Indefinite Past (सामान्य भूत) With तुम and मैं, हो and हूँ are added respectively.

15TH STEP पंद्रहवीं सीढ़ी

TENSE (2)
काल (2)

भूतकाल Past Tense

There are six kinds of Past Tense in Hindi:

(1)	सामान्य भूतकाल	Past Indefinite Tense
(2)	आसन्न भूतकाल	Present Perfect Tense
(3)	पूर्ण भूतकाल	Past Perfect Tense
(4)	संदिग्ध भूतकाल	Past Doubtful Tense
(5)	तात्कालिक भूतकाल	Past Continuous Tense
(6)	हेतुहेतुमद् भूतकाल	Past Conditional Tense

(1) सामान्य भूत *Past Indefinite—*

The past without any definite time or its condition.

The term is formed by adding आ, ए, ई to the root.

सकर्मक क्रिया 'करना'

(Transitive Verb 'to do' Masculine & Feminine

Ist Person —	Singular	मैंने किया	I did
	Plural	हमने किया	We did
IInd Person —	Singular	तूने किया	You did
	Plural	तुमने किया	You did
IIIrd Person —	Singular	उसने किया	He/She did
	Plural	उन्होंने किया	They did

अकर्मक क्रिया 'करना'

(Intransitive Verb 'to laugh' Masculine & Feminine)

Ist Person —	Singular	मैं हँसा/हँसी	I laughed
	Plural	हम हँसे/हँसी	We laughed
IInd Person —	Singular	तू हँसा/हँसी	You laughed
	Plural	तुम हँसे/हँसी	You laughed
IIIrd Person —	Singular	वह हँसा/हँसी	He/She laughed
	Plural	वे हँसे/हँसी	They laughed

(2) आसन्न भूत Present Perfect—

The tense which shows an action just finished—

Examples— मैंने किया है – I have done.

मैं हँसा हूँ – I have laughed.

सकर्मक क्रिया 'करना'

(Transitive Verb 'to do' Masculine & Feminine

Singular : मैंने/तूने/उसने किया है।

Plural : हमने/तुमने/उन्होंने किया है।

अकर्मक क्रिया 'हँसना'

(Intransitive Verb 'to laugh') Masculine & Feminine

Ist Person —	Singular	मैं हँसा हूँ/हँसी हूँ
	Plural	हम हँसे हैं/हँसी हैं
IInd Person —	Singular	तू हँसा है/हँसी है
	Plural	तुम हँसे हो/हँसी हो
IIIrd Person —	Singular	वह हँसा है/हँसी है
	Plural	वे हँसे हैं/हँसी हैं

(3) पूर्ण भूत Past Perfect—

The tense which shows the action finished long ago—

Examples— मैंने किया था – I had done.

मैं हँसा था – I had laughed.

सकर्मक क्रिया 'करना'

(Transitive Verb 'to do') Masculine & Feminine

Singular : मैंने/तूने/उसने-किया था।

Plural : हमने/तुमने/उन्होंने- किया था।

अकर्मक क्रिया 'हँसना'

(Intransitive Verb 'to laugh') Masculine & Feminine

Singular : मैं/तू/वह-हँसा था/हँसी थी।

Plural : हम/तुम/वे- हँसे थे/हँसी थीं।

(4) संदिग्ध भूत Past Doubtful—

An action which might have taken place in the past.

Examples— मैंने किया होगा – I might have done.

मैं हँसा होऊँगा – I might have laughed

सकर्मक क्रिया 'करना'

(Transitive Verb 'to do') Masculine & Feminine

Singular : मैंने/तूने/उसने-किया होगा।

Plural : हमने/तुमने/उन्होंने- किया होगा।

अकर्मक क्रिया 'हँसना'

(Intransitive Verb 'to laugh') Masculine & Feminine

Ist Person —	Singular	मैं हँसा होऊँगा/हँसी होऊँगी
	Plural	हम हँसे होंगे/हँसी होंगी
IInd Person —	Singular	तू हँसा होगा/हँसी होगी
	Plural	तुम हँसे हांगे/हँसी होगी
IIIrd Person —	Singular	वह हँसा होगा/हँसी होगी
	Plural	वे हँसे होंगे/हँसी होंगी

(5) अपूर्ण भूत Past Continuous—

The tense which indicates an action going on in the past.

Examples— मैं कर रहा था – I was doing.

मैं करता था – I was doing.

मैं हँस रहा था – I was laughing

मैं हँसता था – I was laughing

सकर्मक क्रिया 'करना'

(Transitive Verb 'to do') Masculine & Feminine

Singular :	मैं/तू/वह	कर रहा था/करता था।	कर रही थी/करती थी
Plural :	हम/तुम/वे	कर रहे थे/करते थे	कर रही थीं/करती थीं

अकर्मक क्रिया 'हँसना'

(Intransitive Verb 'to laugh', Masculine & Feminine

Singular :	मैं/तू/वह	हँस रहा था/हँसता था।	हँस रही थी/हँसती थी
Plural :	हम/तुम/वे	हँस रहे थे/हँसते थे	हँस रही थीं/हँसती थीं

(6) हेतु हेतु मद् भूत *Past Conditional—*

An action which would have been carried out if a certain condition had been fulfilled in the past. Example:

(यदि) मैं करता.................(If) I had done...................

(यदि) मैं हँसता.................(If) I had laughed..............

सकर्मक क्रिया 'करना'

(Transitive Verb 'to do') Masculine & Feminine

Singular :	(यदि) मैं/तू/वह...	करता............./	करती.............
Plural :	(यदि) हम/तुम/वे...	करता............./	करती.............

अकर्मक क्रिया 'हंसना'

(Intransitive Verb 'to laugh') Masculine & Feminine

Singular :	(यदि) मैं/तू/वह...	हँसता............./	हँसती.............
Plural :	(यदि) हम/तुम/वे...	हँसते............./	हँसती.............

Thus we can conjugate rest to the verbs in all the tenses.

REMARKABLE उल्लेखनीय

The Past Impertect tense indicates two types of actions—

(i) The action which was going on in the past; as—Rakhi was doing it राखी इसे कर रही थी।

(ii) The action which was repeated in the past; as—Rakhi was doing it. राखी इसे (किया) करती थी।

English sentences like 'A king was living in the thick forest', are better translated into Hindi by the past continuous tense:

'A king was living in the thick forest' 'एक राजा घने जंगल में रहता था।' (अर्थात्, रहा करता था)।

16TH STEP सोलहवीं सीढ़ी

VOICE
वाच्य

As we know that there are two kinds of voice in English. But Hindi has three kinds of it, namely:

(i) कर्तृ वाच्य	Active voice
(ii) कर्म वाच्य	Passive voice
(iii) भाव वाच्य	Impersonal voice.

The function of the voice is to show whether in a particular sentence the subject or the object of a verb is prominent.

In the *Active voice,* the importance is given to the subject. For example:

मैं पत्र लिखता हूँ — I write a letter.

In this sentence मैं (subject) is important hence the stress on it. But if object is to be given prominence, the verb gets an additional 'जाना' in the past tense and the subject takes the case-ending से (by). Then it becomes Passive voice.

मुझसे पत्र लिखा जाता है — The Letter is written by me.

In the *Impersonal voice,* the verb used is to be transitive and remains in the third person irrespective of the number and the gender of the object or subject. In the third person its number is always singular and gender masculine.

मैं पढ़ नहीं सकता।	I cannot read.
(Active voice)	
मुझसे पढ़ा नहीं जाता।	I cannot read.
(Impersonal voice)	

Here, पढ़ा the verb holds the main position, Hense the sentence denotes भाव वाच्य।

वाच्य परिवर्तन **Change of voice**

When we change a sentence from the Active voice to the Passive voice, the object of Active voice becomes the subject of the Passive voice and vice versa.

The Passive voice is formed by adding related tense forms of जाना to the past tense and से or द्वारा or के द्वारा with the subject. Examples:

Active	: मैंने फूल तोड़ा।	I pulck the flower.
Possive	: फूल मेरे द्वारा तोड़ा गया।	The flower was plucked by me.
Active	: वह गीत गाती है।	She sings a song.
Passive	: उसके द्वारा गीत गाया गया।	A song is sung by her.
Actice	: राम ने रावण को मारा।	Rama killed Ravana.
Passive	: रावण राम के द्वारा मारा गया।	Ravana was killed by Rama.
Active	: शाहजहां ने ताजमहल बनवाया।	Shahjahan got built Tajmahal.
Passive	: ताजमहल शाहजहां द्वारा बनवाया गया।	Tajmahal was built by Shahjahan.

The Impersonel voice is formed by only intransitive verbs. Example:

Active : घोड़ा नहीं चल सकता। The horse cannot walk.

Impersonel: घोड़े से चला नहीं जाता। The horse cannot walk.

The English version of the Impersonel voice is the same as Active voice, because in English, there is no Impersonel voice.

REMARKABLE उल्लेखनीय

भाव वाच्य or Impersonal voice is found rare. It is mostly used negatively to express inability. Here the main verb does not change in any way and remains singular, masculine, past participle position (पढ़ा, लिखा, सोया, चला, etc.) उससे चला नहीं जाता। मुझसे जिया नहीं जाता। रोगी से सोया नहीं जाता। These sentences cannot be translated into English in the same tone, because, sentences containing an intransitive verb do not admit of a passive voice in English. The meaning of the above sentence is 'I am unable to walk. I cannot live. The patient cannot sleep'.

17TH STEP सत्रहवीं सीढ़ी

THE KINDS OF SECONDARY VERBS
यौगिक क्रियाओं के प्रकार

1. प्रेरणार्थक क्रिया Causal Verb

प्रेरणार्थक क्रिया (Causal verb) shows an effect to cause others to do. Example:

(i) यह पत्र मीनाक्षी से लिखवाओ।	Get this letter written by Minakshi.
(ii) मैंने धोबी से कपड़े इस्तरी करवाए।	I got the cloth pressed by the washerman.

These are causal verbs लिखवाओ, करवाए (forms of लिखवाना and करवाना) in the above sentences.

Most of the verbs in Hindi have two Causal verbs. The first one shows the immediate causation and the second one remoteness. Example: पढ़ना (to read), पढ़ाना (to make read), पढ़वाना (to cause to read).

There are certain rules in forming the Causal verb. Those may be watched and learnt and understand.

(a) No change occurs in roots. Examples:

Root	Infinitive	Ist Causative	2nd Causative
	[–ना]	[–आना]	[–पाना]
कर	करना	कराना	करवाना

पढ़	पढ़ना	पढ़ाना	पढ़वाना
सुन	सुनना	सुनाना	सुनवाना
लिख	लिखना	लिखाना	लिखवाना
उठ	उठना	उठाना	उठवाना

(b) The first vowel of two lettered roots is shortened: आ to अ/ई-ए-ऐ to इ/ऊ-ओ-औ to उ। Examples:

Root	Infinitive	Ist Causative	2nd Causative
बोल	बोलना	बुलाना	बुलवाना
जाग	जागना	जगाना	जगवाना
जीत	जीतना	जिताना	जितवाना
लेट	लेटना	लिटाना	लिटवाना
खोद	खोदना	खुदाना	खुदवाना

(c) Roots ending in long vowels have ल before causal addition. Example:

Root	Infinitive	Ist Causative	2nd Causative
खा	खाना	खिलाना	खिलवाना
सी	सीना	सिलाना	सिलवाना
दे	देना	दिलाना	दिलवाना
पी	पीना	पिलाना	पिलवाना
रो	रोना	रुलाना	रुलवाना

It is worth remembering that some verbs do not form causals. That are as follows—

आना	जाना	पाना	सकना
होना	पड़ना	रहना	सुस्ताना
लजाना	कुम्हलाना		

2. सहायक क्रिया Auxiliary verb

सहायक क्रिया (Auxiliary verb) helps to form a tense or mood of some principal verb. While conjugating, changes occurs in auxiliary verb and the principal verb remain unchanged.

चुक and पड़ are independent verbs, but they can also be used as helping verbs in Hindi. Indeclinable चाहिए can also be used as helping verb.

(a) **सकना** *(to express ability or permission):*

(i) हम इसे अपने-आप हल कर सकते है।	We can slove it ourselves. (Ability)
(ii) मैं हिंदी पढ़ और लिख सकता हूँ।	I can read and write Hindi. (Ability)
(iii) क्या मैं अंदर आ सकता हूँ, श्रीमान?	May I come in, Sir? (Permission)
(iv) अब आप जा सकते है।	Now you can go. (Permission)

(b) **चुकना** *(to express completion of an action):*

(i) हम सब खाना खा चुके हैं।	All of us have taken our meal.
(ii) नेताजी पहले ही आ चुके थे।	Nataji had already come.

(c) **चाहिए** *(to denote duty, determination or moral obligation)– In the sense of* चाहिए *'should', 'must' or 'ought to' are used in English:*

(i) प्रत्येक को अपना कर्त्तव्य निभाना चाहिए।	One must keep one's duty.
(ii) आपको भगवद्गीता पढ़नी चाहिए।	You should read the Bhagwat Gita.
(iii) तुम्हें बड़ों का सम्मान करना चाहिए था।	You ought to have respected your elders.

(d) **पढ़ना** *(to express the sense of helplessness and necessity):*

(i) हमें मद्रास जाना पड़ा।	We had to go to Madras.
(ii) उसे रोज यहां आना पड़ता है।	He has to come here daily.

3. संयुक्त क्रिया Compound verb

संयुक्त क्रिया (Compound verb) is the combination of two basic roots to intensify the meaning.

In compound verb, one root is principal while the other is

secondary one. The root of the principal verb does not change while the subordinate root is conjugated in the usual way.

The subordinate verb does not give its ful meaning, but modifies the meaning of prinicipal verb.

Here are some verbs which are used as the secondary verbs of the compound verbs. The verbs are– रखना, लेना, देना, जाना, डालना, रहना, पाना, बैठना, उठना, भागना, देखना, etc.

(a) **रहना** *denotes the sense of continuation of an incomplete action; as—*

खेलती रहती है   हँसता रहता है   लड़ते रहते हैं

वाक्य–हम चलते रहते हैं। We keep walking.

(b) **उठना** *expresses suddenness of action; as—*

जाग उठी   रो उठा   चिल्ला उठे

वाक्य–वह बहुत चिंतित हो उठा He become very anxious.

(c) **जाना** *expresses completeness (of principal verb); as—*

बैठ जाता है   सो जाएगा   डूब गया

वाक्य–वह मेज पर खड़ा हो गया। He stood up on the table.

(d) **बैठना** *shows an element of unaware action; as—*

उठ बैठा है   लड़ बैठी है   कर बैठे हैं

वाक्य–मैं अपना पैन खो बैठा हूँ। I had lost my pen.

(e) **पाना** *shows ability to complete anything. Subjoined verb* पाना *is oftenly used in negative sentences; as—*

कर (नहीं) पाया   दे (नहीं) पाया   बैठ (नहीं) पाये

वाक्य–मैं नींद नहीं कर पाया। I could not sleep.

REMARKABLE उल्लेखनीय

चाहिए is used in the meaning of 'is wanted' or 'ought to be...' It can be combined with a noun in first sense, and with an infinitive in the second sense. As:

(A)	हमें मिठाई चाहिए।	We want sweetmeat (literally speaking, sweetmeat is wanted by us).
	हमें मिठाइयाँ चाहिए।	We want sweetmeats.
	उसे क्या चाहिए?	What does she want? (literally speaking, what is wanted by her.)
	उसे पेंसिलें चाहिए।	She wants pencils (literally, Pencils' are wanted by her.)
(B)	आपको सोना चाहिए।	You ought to sleep. (infinitive noun)
	हमें रोज सैर करनी चाहिए।	We ought to walk daily.

N. B. The plural form of चाहिए could be चाहिएँ। But now चाहिएँ is treated as an old usage. In modern Hindi चाहिए is unchangeable form, in both, the singular and the plural.

18TH STEP अठारहवीं सीढ़ी

INDECLINABLE
अव्यय या अविकारी

The words which remain always unchangeable are called अव्यय or अविकारी शब्द (Indeclinable), as— आज (today), कल (tomorrow), जल्दी (quickly), यहां (here), वहां (there), etc.

There are four types of indeclinable words—

1. क्रियाविशेषण	Adverb
2. संबंधबोधक	Post-position
3. समुच्चयबोधक	Conjunction
4. विस्मयादिबोधक	Exclamation

Now we shall discuss them briefly.

1. **क्रियाविशेषण Aderb**: *(A word which mostly qualifies a verb)*:

(i) अमित नहीं आएगा।	Amit will not come.
(ii) तुम्हारे पास कितना समय है?	How much time have you?
(iii) वह कैसे लिखता है?	How does he write?
(iv) कहां जा रहे हो?	Where are you going?
(v) अब गाना शुरू करो।	Now start singing.

In the above sentences नहीं, कितना, कैसे, कहां, अब are adverbs, because each of them qualifies its verb. All these are अव्यय:

स्थानसूचक - कहाँ, यहाँ, वहाँ, जहाँ, किधर।

रीतिसूचक - धीरे-धीरे, कैसे।

निषेधसूचक - मत, नहीं, न।

कालसूचक - अब, जब, तब, कब, तुरंत।

परिमाणसूचक-उतना, इतना, जितना, कितना।

2. **संबंधबोधक Post-position** *(A word which shows relation of noun, pronoun, etc., with other words of the sentence):*

(i) मेज पर पुस्तक पड़ी है।	The book is on the table.
(ii) विकास पीछे रह गया।	Vikas has trailed behind.
(iii) आपके समान बहादुर कोई नहीं।	There is no one brave like you
(iv) तुम मेरे खिलाफ जा रहे हो।	You are going against me.
(v) यह केवल आपके लिए है।	It is only for you.

In the above sentences पर, पीछे, (के) समान, खिलाफ और (के) लिए are post-positions.

The following are post-positions:

स्थानसूचक - (के) भीतर, पर, में; (से) दूर, निकट, ऊपर; (के) आगे, पीछे।

कालसूचक - (के) आगे, पीछे; (के) पश्चात्; उपरांत; (से) पहले।

समतासूचक - (के) समान, बराबर, जैसा, सा, (की) भांति।

विरोधसूचक - (के) प्रतिकूल, विरुद्ध, खिलाफ।

कारण बोधक - (के) लिए, (के) कारण, हेतु।

अन्य-को, (की) ओर, (के) प्रति (दिशाबोधक); (से) दूर, से (पृथकतासूचक); (के) सहारे, द्वारा (साधनसूचक)

It must be noticed that संबंधबोधक are called post-positions (against English Preposition) because they come after the words qualified by them.

3. **समुच्चयबोधक Conjunction** *(A word which is used to join sentences, words or clauses):*

(i) डबलरोटी और मक्खन पर्याप्त आहार है।	Bread and butter is a sufficient food.
(ii) मुझे बुखार हो गया है, इसलिए मैं उपस्थित नहीं हो सकता।	I am suffering from fever so I cannot attend.
(iii) तुम यहां आओगे कि नहीं?	Will you come here or not?

In the above sentences, और (and) इसलिए (so), कि (or) are conjunctions, which join respectively words and sentences.

The following are conjuctions—

(i) और एवं, तथा;

(ii) अथवा, या नहीं तो;

(iii) इसलिए, अतएव, क्योंकि;

(iv) यदि- तो, यद्यपि- तो भी;

(v) अर्थात्, जैसे कि;

(vi) पर, परंतु, किंतु, बल्कि;

(vii) ताकि।

4. **विस्मयादिबोधक** *Exclamation (A word which expresses an exclamatory feeling or emotion of the speaker):*

(i) वाह-वाह, मैंने प्रथम पुरस्कार जीता।	Hurrah! won the first prize.
(ii) अहा! यह बाग कितना सुंदर है।	Oh! what a beautiful garden it is!
(iii) अरे! वह मर गया।	Ah, he expired!
(iv) हाय! मैं अब क्या करूं।	Alas, what shall I do now!

In the above sentences, वाह-वाह, अहा, अरे, हाय are the words which expresses the feelings of joy, surprise and sorrow. All these are exclamations.

List of exclamation—

विस्मय	-	अरे! ओह!
उत्साह	-	धन्य! शाबाश!
आनंद	-	वाह-वाह! अहा!
दुख	-	ओह! हाय!
संबोधन	-	ओ! अरी-री! अरे, रे! अजी!
घृणा	-	छिः-छिः ऊँह! धत्!
विवशता	-	काश!

REMARKABLE उल्लेखनीय

	(A)	(B)
(i)	बुरा मत कहो	बुरा न कहो
(ii)	बुरा मत सुनो	बुरा न सुनो
(iii)	बुरा मत देखो	बुरा न देखो

In the above sentences, there is some difference. In the first column, मत is in negative sense, but in the second, न is substituted.

Roughly speaking, sentences of column A & B have the similar meanings. But actually it is not correct.

मत is used when we want to give much force or stress to our order in the imperative mood. Remember, in case of putting न instead, the stress lessened in some extent.

19TH STEP उन्नीसवीं सीढ़ी

CARDINAL NUMERALS (GINTI)
गिनती

1. एक	24. चौबीस	47. सैंतालीस	70. सत्तर
2. दो	25. पच्चीस	48. अड़तालीस	71. इकहत्तर
3. तीन	26. छब्बीस	49. उनचास	72. बहत्तर
4. चार	27. सत्ताईस	50. पचास	73. तिहत्तर
5. पांच	28. अट्ठाईस	51. इकयावन	74. चौहत्तर
6. छः	29. उनतीस	52. बावन	75. पचहत्तर
7. सात	30. तीस	53. तिरेपन	76. छिहत्तर
8. आठ	31. इकत्तीस	54. चौवन	77. सतहत्तर
9. नौ	32. बत्तीस	55. पचपन	78. अठहत्तर
10. दस	33. तैंतीस	56. छप्पन	79. उनासी
11. ग्यारह	34. चौंतीस	57. सत्तावन	80. अस्सी
12. बारह	35. पैंतीस	58. अट्ठावन	81. इकयासी
13. तेरह	36. छत्तीस	59. उनसठ	82. बयासी
14. चौदह	37. सैंतीस	60. साठ	83. तिरासी
15. पंद्रह	38. अड़तीस	61. इकसठ	84. चौरासी
16. सोलह	39. उन्तालीस	62. बासठ	85. पचासी
17. सत्रह	40. चालीस	63. तिरसठ	86. छियासी
18. अठारह	41. इकतालीस	64. चौंसठ	87. सत्तासी
19. उन्नीस	42. बयालीस	65. पैंसठ	88. अट्ठासी
20. बीस	43. तैतालीस	66. छियासठ	89. नवासी
21. इक्कीस	44. चवालीस	67. सड़सठ	90. नब्बे
22. बाईस	45. पैंतालीस	68. अड़सठ	91. इकयानवे
23. तेईस	46. छियालीस	69. उनहत्तर	92. बानवे

93. तेरानवे	95. पचानवे	97. सत्तानवे	99. निन्यानवे
94. चौरानवे	96. छियानवे	98. अट्ठानवे	100. सौ

1,000 हजार 1,00,000 लाख

1,00,00,000 करोड़

Ordinals क्रमांक (Kramank)

1st	पहला	6th	छठा
2st	दूसरा	7th	सातवाँ
3rd	तीसरा	8th	आठवाँ
4th	चौथा	9th	नवाँ
5th	पाँचवाँ	10th	दसवाँ

Multiplicative numerals गुणनांक (Guṇanāṅk)

Twofold	दुगुना	Sevenfold	सतगुना
Threefold	तिगुना	Eightfold	अठगुना
Fourfold	चौगुना	Ninefold	नौगुना
Fivefold	पचगुना	Tenfold	सतगुना
Sixfold	छहगुना		

Frequentative numerals आवृत्तिपरक अंक (Āvrattipark Aṅk)

Once	एक बार	Four time	चार बार
Twice	दो बार	Five time	पांच बार
Thrice	तीन बार		

Aggregative numerals
पूर्णयोगांक (Purṇayogaṅk)

Both	दोनों	All twenty	बीसों
All three	तीनों	Scores of	बीसियों
All four	चारों	Hundreds of	सैकड़ों
All ten	दसों	Thousands of	हजारों

REMARKABLE उल्लेखनीय

1. The numerals 11 to 18 ending in—ah (-अह) have common variant pronounciations with long a, i.e., ग्यारह (ग्यारह), पंद्रह (पंदरा), etc.
2. In similar ending pronunciation, उन्नीस (19) is nearer to बीस (20), उनतीस (29) to तीस (30), उनतालीस (39), to चालीस (40), उनचास (49), to पचास (50) and so on.
3. हजार and सहस्र (thousand) are usually used as nouns and prefixed by एक etc.

20TH STEP बीसवीं सीढ़ी

ERRORS IN SPELLINGS
वर्तनी की भूलें

There are some examples of incorrect and correct forms of words, which are mostly mistaken by common men. Try to follow the correct forms of words.

Incorred	*Correct*	*Incorrect*	*Correct*
अवश्यक	आवश्यक	दुख	दु:ख
अत्याधिक	अत्यधिक	हिन्दु	हिन्दू
अगनि	अग्नि	जन्ता	जनता
औद्योगिकरण	उद्योगीकरण	प्रथक	पृथक
उज्जवल	उज्ज्वल	कृप्या	कृपया
उपरोक्त	उपर्युक्त	रात्री	रात्रि
आर्शीवाद	आशीर्वाद	बहु	बहू
उपलक्ष	उपलक्ष्य	शुरु	शुरू
एतिहासिक	ऐतिहासिक	गुरू	गुरु
कवियित्री	कवयित्री	पुज्य	पूज्य
चिन्ह	चिह्न	ऐैसा	ऐसा
सन्यासी	संन्यासी	लघू	लघु
प्रतिछाया	प्रतिच्छाया	घन्टी	घण्टी
प्रीक्षा	परीक्षा	श्रेष्ट	श्रेष्ठ
श्रीमति	श्रीमती	सतत्	सतत

चरम	चरम	पुन्य	पुण्य
कुरुप	कुरूप	प्रभू	प्रभु
सहस्त्र	सहस्र	स्त्रि	स्त्री
स्वास्थ	स्वास्थ्य	प्रती	प्रति
हंसना	हँसना	कहां	कहाँ
वायू	वायु	हूं	हूँ
प्रन्तु	परन्तु	जै	जय
अत:एव	अतएव	रतन	रत्न
पूज्यनीय	पूजनीय	प्रन	प्रण
कठनाई	कठिनाई	दृष्य	दृश्य
जाग्रत	जागृत	पत्नि	पत्नी
पश्चाताप	पश्चात्ताप	स्वामि	स्वामी
दुरदशा	दुर्दशा	रीती	रीति
श्रंगार	शृंगार	तिथी	तिथि
सौन्दर्यता	सौन्दर्य	कृया	क्रिया
समुन्दर	समुद्र	हन्स	हंस
परिवारिक	पारिवारिक	आंख	आँख
बिमार	बीमार	कुपूत	कपूत
कृपालू	कृपालु	पृष्ट	पृष्ठ
अम्रित	अमृत	सपुत्र	सुपुत्र
क्रिषक	कृषक	शरधा	श्रद्धा
प्राधीन	पराधीन	ग्यान	ज्ञान
पुर्नजन्म	पुनर्जन्म	टेड़ा	टेढ़ा
सन्मुख	सम्मुख	बूड़ा	बूढ़ा
लोकिक	लौकिक	पुष्ठ	पुष्ट
आधीन	अधीन	सन्शय	संशय
स्थायि	स्थायी	हिन्सा	हिंसा
पन्डित	पंडित	हन्स	हंस
निर्दोषी	निर्दोष	कुत्तिया	कुतिया
शांतमय	शांतिमय	कुता	कुत्ता

विशवास	विश्वास	निर्दयी	निर्दय
उपयोगता	उपयोगिता	टेड़ा	टेढ़ा
ठकुराईन	ठकुराइन	बूड़ा	बूढ़ा
निरपराधी	निरपराध	कृतग्य	कृतज्ञ
अभिनेत्रि	अभिनेत्री	पड़ाई	पढ़ाई
स्थायीत्व	स्थायित्व	बड़ई	बढ़ई
औढ़ना	ओढ़ना	नीती	नीति
द्वितिय	द्वितीय	औढ़ना	ओढ़ना
सतारह	सत्रह	क्रिपा	कृपा
नवम्	नवम	ऐक	एक
सड़ीयल	सड़ियल	रूपया	रुपया
भारतिय	भारतीय	सोतैला	सौतेला
दुगुणा	दुगुना	क्रिषी	कृषि
पांडीत्य	पांडित्य	सपुत्र	सुपुत्र
स्त्रीयां	स्त्रियाँ	यथेष्ठ	यथेष्ट
दुरावस्था	दुरवस्था	ज्योती	ज्योति
इकठ्ठा	इक्ट्ठा	संसारिक	सांसारिक
कौशलता	कौशल	ज्योत्सना	ज्योत्स्ना

REMARKABLE उल्लेखनीय

1. The pronunciation of ऋ is very near to the pronunciation of ri in English word **bridge.** Its pronunciation is somewhere between अ and ई– nearer to इ. So that कृपा is not exactly क्रिपा kripa but krupa.
2. In pronunciation कृषि is different from क्रिषि in the same way, as क्रिया is different from कृया। In both the examples, the second one are incorrect.

PART 3
CLASSIFIED SENTENCES

21ST STEP इक्कीसवी सीढ़ी

USEFUL EXPERESSIONS
उपयोगी लघु वाक्य

We can convey our thoughts and feelings through small phrases and sentences. Let us learn to speak briefly.

Here are some phrases and short sentences:

1. Hello!	अहो!	Aho!
2. Happy New year!	नव वर्ष की शुभकामना!	Nav Varṣa ki shubhkāmnā!
3. Same to you!	आपको भी!	Āpko bhī.
4. Happy birthday to you!	जन्मदिन मुबारक!	Janmadin mubārak!
5. Welcome you all!	आप सब का स्वागत!	Ap sab kā swāgat!
6. Congratulations!	बधाई हो!	Badhaī ho!
7. Thanks for your kind visit.	आपके पधारने का धन्यवाद!	Āpke padhārne kā dhanyavād.
8. Thank God!	भगवान् का धन्यवाद है!	Bhagwān kā dhanyavād hai!
9. Oh my darling!	ओ मेरे प्रिय!	Oh mere priya!
10. O God!	हे राम	He Rām!
11. Oh!	अरे!	Are!

12. Bravo!	क्या खूब!	Kya Khūb!
13. Woe!	हाय!	Hāye!
14. Excellent!	क्या खूब!	kyā khūb!
15. How terrible!	कितना डरावना!	Kitnā darāvanā!
16. How absurd!	कितना भौंडा!	kitnā bhaunda!
17. How beautiful!	कितना सुंदर!	Kitna sundar!
18. How disqraceful!	कितना लज्जा-जनक!	Kitnā lajjajanak!
19. Really!	सच!	Sach!
20. O.K.	अच्छा!	Achchha!
21. Wonderfull!	अद्‌भुत!	Adbhut!
22. Thank you!	आपका धन्यवाद!	Apkā dhanyavād!
23. Certainly!	निस्संदेह	Nissandeh!
24. What a great victory!	कितनी महान विजय!	Kitni mahān vijay!
25. With best compliments!	अभिनंदन के साथ!	Abhinandan ke sāth!

Some useful clauses and short sentences:

1. Just a minute.	जरा एक मिनट	Jara ek minaṭ!
2. Just coming.	अभी आया।	Abhi āyā.
3. Any more?	कुछ और?	Kuchḥ aur?
4. Enough.	काफी है।	Kāfi hai.
5. Anything else?	और कुछ?	Aur kuchh?
6. No worry.	कोई चिंता नहीं।	Koi chintā nahiṅ.
7. As you like.	जैसी आपकी इच्छा।	Jaisi apki ichchā!
8. Mention not.	कोई बात नहीं।	Koi bāt nahin!
9. Nothing more.	और कुछ नहीं।	Aur kuchh nahin!

10. Not at all.	कदापि नहीं।	Kadāpi nahin.
11. For ladies	महिलाओं के लिए।	Mahilāon ke liya.
12. To let	किराये के लिए खाली है।	Kirāye ke liya khāli hai.
13. No admission.	प्रवेश वर्जित है।	Pravesh varjit hai.
14. No entrance.	प्रवेश नहीं।	Pravesh nahain.
15. No thoroughfare.	आम रास्ता नहीं है।	Am rāstā nahin hai.
16. No talking.	बातचीत करना मना है।	Batchit karnā manā hai.
17. No smoking.	सिगरेट पीना मना है।	Sigret pinā manā hai.
18. No spitting.	थूकना मना है।	Thūknā manā hai.
19. No parking.	वाहन खड़ा करना वर्जित है।	Vāhan khaṛa karnā varjit hai.
20. No exit	बाहर जाना मना है।	Bāhar jājā manā hai.

22ND STEP बाईसवीं सीढ़ी

IMPERATIVE SENTENCES
विध्यर्थक वाक्य

In the following sentences, there are many verbs in the imperative mood expressing order, request for advice.

Here are some examples of short sentences giving force to verbs.

1. The Sentences Indicating Order:

1. Be quick.	जल्दी करो।	Jaldi karo.
2. Be quiet.	चुप रहो!	Chup raho.
3. Come in.	अंदर आओ।	Andar āo.
4. Get out.	बाहर निकल जाओ।	Bāhar nikal jāo.
5. Stick no bills.	इश्तहार मत लगाओ।	Ishtahār mat lagāo.
6. Don't talk rot.	बकवास मत करो।	Bakvās mat karo.
7. Be careful	सावधान रहो।	Savdhān raho.
8. Bring a glass of water.	एक गिलास पानी लाओ।	Ek gilās pāni lāo.
9. Don't forget to come tomorrow.	कल आना मत भूलो।	Kal ānā mat bhūlo.
10. Don't haste.	हड़बड़ी मत करो।	Harbaṛi mat karo.
11. Don't be talkative.	बातूनी मत बनो।	Batuni mat bano.

12. Speak the truth.	सच बोलो।	Sach bolo.
13. Don't tell a lie.	झूठ मत बोलो।	Jhūṭh mat bolo.
14. Go back.	वापस जाओ।	Vāpas jāo.
15. Work hard.	परिश्रम करो।	Parishram karo.
16. Shut the window	खिड़की बंद करो।	Khiṛki band karo.
17. Open the door.	दरवाज़ा खोलो।	Darwajā kholo.
18. Come forward.	आगे आओ।	Āge āo.
19. Come alone.	अकेले आओ।	Akele āo.
20. Sit down.	बैठ जाओ।	Baiṭh jāo.
21. Stand up.	खड़े हो जाओ।	Khaṛe ho jāo.
22. Get up early.	जल्दी उठो।	Jaldi uṭho.
23. Be ready by 8 o' clock.	आठ बजे तक तैयार रहो।	Āṭh baje tak taiyār raho.
24. Always keep to the left.	सदा बायें चलो।	Sadā bayeṅ chalo.
25. Give up bad habits.	बुरी आदतें छोड़ों।	Buri ādateṅ chhoṛo.
26. Mind your own business.	अपना काम देखो।	Apnā kām dekho.
27. Ring the bell.	घंटी बजाओ।	Ghanṭi bajāo.
28. Take it away.	इसे ले जाओ।	Ise le jāo.
29. Return the balance.	बाकी पैसे लौटा दो।	Bāki paise lautā do.

2. The Sentences Indicating Request:

30. Please, excuse me	क्षमा करें।	Kshamā kareṅ.
31. Don't mind, please.	बुरा मत मानिए।	Burā mat māniye.
32. Please, try to understand me.	मुझे समझने का यत्न करें।	Mujhe samajhne kā yatna kareṅ.

33. Please, lend me your bicycle.	कृपया मुझे अपनी साइकिल दीजिए।	Kripayā mujhe apni sāikal dijiye.
34. Follow me, please.	मेरे पीछे आइए।	Mere pichhe aiye.
35. Please, have a cold drink.	कुछ ठण्डा लीजिए।	Kuchh ṭhanḍa lijiye.
36. Have some coffee, please	थोड़ी-सी काफी लीजिए।	Thori si kofi lijiye na.
37. Please, have the room swept.	कृपया कमरे में सफाई करवा दीजिए।	Kripaya kamre meṅ safāi karvā dijiye.
38. Please, call the servant.	नौकर को बुलाइए न।	Naukar ko bulāiya na.
39. Please, pass me the chilly.	मिर्च पकड़ाइए न।	Mirch pakṛāiye na.
40. Please, bring us some sweets.	हमारे लिए कुछ मिठाई लाइए।	Hamāre liya kuchh miṭhāi lāiye.
41. Please deliver the goods at my residence.	कृपया ये वस्तुएं मेरे आवास पर पहुंचवा दीजिए।	Kripaya ye vastueṅ mere āvās par pahunchavā dijiye.
42. Please take your bath.	स्नान कर लीजिए।	Snān kar lijiye.
43. Please have your seat.	अपनी जगह पर बैठिए।	Apni jagah par baiṭhiye.
44. Kindly inform in time.	समय पर सूचित करें।	samay par sūchit karen.
45. Kindly grant me a loan.	कृपा करके मुझे ऋण प्रदान करें।	Kripā karke mujhe riṇ pradān kareṅ.

3. The Sentences Indicating Advice:

46. Let us go in time.	हमें समय पर ज़ाना चाहिए।	Hemeṅ samay par jānā chāhiye.

47.	Work hard lest you will fail.	मेहनत करो नहीं तो विफल हो जाओगे।	Mehnat karo nahiṅ to viphal ho jāoge.
48.	Let us wait.	हम इन्तज़ार कर लें।	Ham intzār kar leṅ.
49.	Let us go for a walk.	आओ सैर करें।	Ao sair kareṅ.
50.	Let us make the best use of time.	आओ समय का सदुपयोग करें।	Ao samy kā sadupyog kareṅ.
51.	Let us try our best.	आओ हम अपना पूरा यत्न करे।	Āo ham apnā pūrā yatna kareṅ.
52.	Let it be so.	चलने दीजिए।	Chalne dijiye
53.	Let us think first over this matter.	आओ पहले इस विषय पर विचार कर लें।	Āo pahle is visay par vichār kar leṅ.
54.	Let us go to cinema together.	आओ इकट्ठे सिनेमा चलें।	Ao ikaṭṭhe sinema chaleṅ.

23RD STEP तेईसवीं सीढ़ी

PRESENT TENSE
वर्तमान काल

1. Present Indefinite Tense सामान्य वर्तमान

1.	I write a letter to my brother.	मैं अपने भाई को पत्र लिखता हूँ।	Main apne bhāi ko patra likhtā huṅ.
2.	Some children like sweets.	कुछ बच्चे मिठाई पसंद करते हैं।	Kuchh bachche miṭhāi pasand karte hain.
3.	I leave home at 9.00 a.m. everyday.	मैं प्रतिदिन नौ बजे घर से चलता हूँ।	Maiñ pratidin nau baje ghar se chaltā hūṅ.
4.	The earth moves round the sun	पृथ्वी सूर्य के चारों ओर घूमती है।	Prithvī sūrya ke chāroṅ or ghūmti hai.
5.	Good child always obeys his parents.	अच्छा बच्चा सदा अपने माता-पिता का कहना मानता है।	Achchhā bachchā sadā apne mātā-pitā kā kahnā māntā hai.
6.	She drives too quickly.	वह बहुत तेज गाड़ी चलाती है।	Vah bahut tez gāri chalāti hai.
7.	I brush my teeth	मैं अपने दांत दिन	Maiṅ apne dānt din

twice a day.	में दो बार साफ करता हूं।	meṅ do bār sāf karta huṅ.
8. We live in India.	हम भारत में रहते हैं।	Ham Bhārat meṅ rahte haiṅ.
9. You always forget to pay.	तुम सदा पैसे चुकाना भूल जाते हो।	Tum sada paise chukānā bhūl jāte ho.
10. The last bus leaves at midnight.	आखिरी बस आधी रात को छूटती है।	Akhiri bas ādhi rat ko chhutati hai.
11. You spend all your money on clothes.	तुम अपना सारा पैसा कपड़ों पर खर्च कर देते हो।	Tum apnā sārā paisā kapṛoṅ par kharcha kar deta ho.
12. Someone knocks at the door.	कोई दरवाजा खटखटाता है।	Koi darwāzā khaṭkhatāta hai.
13. She always wears the glasses.	वह हर समय ऐनक पहनती है।	Vah har samay ainak pahantī hai.
14. In India, there fifteen regional languages.	भारत में पन्द्रह क्षेत्रीय भाषाएं हैं।	Bhārat meṅ paṅdrah kshetriy bhāsāyeṅ hain.

2. *Present Continuous Tense* तात्कालिक वर्तमान

1. My mother is sweeping the room.	मेरी माताजी कमरा साफ कर रही हैं।	Meri mātāji kamrā sāf kar rahi haiṅ.
2. I am reading Nav Bharat Times.	मैं नवभारत टाइम्स पढ़ रहा हूं।	Main Nav Bharat Times paṛh raha huṅ.

3. The dog is lying under the car.	कुत्ता कार के नीचे लेट रहा है।	Kuttā kār ke niche leṭ rahā hai.
4. He is going to the market.	वह बाजार जा रहा है।	Vah bazār jā rahā hai.
5. She is crying for nothing.	वह बेकार में शोर मचा रही है।	Vah bekār meṅ shor machā rahi hāi.
6. I am just coming.	मैं अभी आ रहा हूं।	Maiṅ abhi ā rahā huṅ.
7. I am looking at the sky.	मैं आसमान की ओर देख रहा हूं।	Maiṅ āsmān ki or dekh rahā huṅ.
8. I am singing the song.	मैं गाना गा रही हूं।	Main gānā ga rahi huṅ.
9. She is looking for a pen.	वह पेन ढूंढ़ रही है।	Vah pen dhūṅḍh rahi hai.
10. The patient is going to the hospital.	रोगी अस्पताल जा रहा है।	Rogi aspatāl ja rahā hai.

3. *Doubtful Present Tense* संदिग्ध वर्तमान

1. She may be reaching her office.	वह अपने कार्यालय पहुंच रही होगी।	Vah apne kāryālay pahunch rahi hogi.
2. They may be thinking wrong.	वे गलत सोचते होंगे।	Ve galat sochte honge.
3. I may be going to Bombay tomorrow.	मैं कल बम्बई पहुंच रहा होऊंगा।	Main kal Bambai pahunch raha hoūṅgā.
4. I may be teaching Hindi to my pupils.	मैं अपने छात्रों को हिंदी पढ़ा रहा होऊंगा।	Main apne chātroṅ ko Hindi pardhā rahā hoūṅgā.

5. Your sister may be waiting for you.	आपकी बहन आपका इंतजार कर रही होगी।	Āpki bahen āpkā iṅṭzār kar rahi hogi.
6. She may be playing on the voilin.	वह वायलिन बजाती होगी।	Vah vayelin bajati hogi.
7. She may be returning the money in a week.	वह सप्ताह-भर में पैसा लौटाती होगी।	Vah saptāh-bhar men paisa lauṭāti hogi.
8. Rama may be learning her lesson in the morning.	रमा प्रातःकाल अपना पाठ याद करती होगी।	Ramā prāta:kāl apnā pāth yād karti hogi.

24TH STEP चौबीसवीं सीढ़ी

FUTURE TENSE
भविष्यत्काल

1. *Future Indefinite Tense* सामान्य भविष्यत्काल

1. I shall write a letter to my brother.	मैं अपने भाई को पत्र लिखूंगा।	Main apne bhāi ko patra likhūṅgā.
2. My father will reach here by Sunday	मेरे पिताजी रविवार तक यहां पहुंच जायेंगे।	Mere pitāji ravivar tak yahāṅ pahuṅch jāyeṅge.
3. The mother will go to the market tomorrow.	माताजी कल बाजार जायेंगी।	Mātaji kal bazār jāyeṅgi.
4. She will study hard this year.	वह इस वर्ष कड़ी मेहनत से पढ़ाई करेगी।	Vah ish varṣa kaṛi mehnat se paṛhāi karegi.
5. It will serve my purpose.	इससे मेरा काम चल जायेगा।	Isase merā kām chal jāyegā.
6. I shall return day after tomorrow.	मैं परसों लौट जाऊंगा।	Main parson lauṭ jāoṅgā.
7. My brother will stay here at night.	मेरा भाई रात को यहां ठहर जाएगा।	Merā bhāi rāt ko yahān ṭhahar jāyegā.

8. I shall return in the evening definitely.	मैं शाम को निश्चित रूप से लौट जाऊंगा।	Maiṅ shām ko nishchit rūp se lauṭ jaūṅgā.
9. I will do it whatever happens.	जो कुछ भी हो, मैं इसे अवश्य करूंगा।	Jo kuchh bhī ho, maiṅ ise avashya karūṅgā.
10. I will certainly give you what you want.	जो कुछ आप चाहेंगे, मैं आपको निश्चित रूप से दूंगा।	Jo kuchh āp cāheṅge, maiṅ āpko nishchit rūp se dūṅgā.
11. We shall start at about 5 o'clock.	हम लगभग पांच बजे चलेंगे।	Ham lagbhag pañch baje chaleṅge.
12. I will give up smoking definitely.	मैं निश्चित रूप से धूम्रपान छोड़ दूंगा।	Main nischit rūp se dhumrapān chhoṛ dūṅgā.
13. I will come positively.	मैं अवश्य आऊंगा।	Maiṅ avashya āūṅgā.
14. I will see it later on.	मैं इसे बाद में देखूंगा।	Maiṅ ise bād meiṅ dekhūṅgā.

2. Contingent Future Tense संभाव्य भविष्यत्

1. If your elder brother come you do come.	यदि तुम्हारे भाई साहब आयें तो तुम भी जरूर आना।	Yadi tumhāre bhāi āyeṅ to tum bhi zarūr ānā.
2. If you stay I do stay.	यदि तुम ठहरो तो मैं भी ठहरूं।	Yadi tum ṭhahro to maiṅ bhi ṭhahrūṅ.
3. Ranjana may arrive today.	शायद रंजना आज पहुंचे।	Shāyad Rañjanā āj pahuṅche.
4. I may invite my	संभवतः मैं अपने	Sambhavtah maiṅ

colleagues also.	साथियों को भी बुलाऊं।	apne sāthioṅ ko bhi bulāūṅ.
5. If you go for a walk, call me also.	यदि तुम सैर को जाओ तो मुझे भी बुलाना।	Yadi tum sair ko jāo to mujhe bhi bulānā.
6. You may rest in my cottage if you like.	यदि तुम चाहो तो मेरी कुटिया में आराम कर लो।	Yadi tum cāho to meri kutiyā meiṅ ārām kar lo.
7. I may leave this station any time.	मैं कभी भी यह स्टेशन छोड़ दूं।	Maiṅ kabhi bhi yah steshan choṛ duṅ.
8. She may attend the meeting tomorrow.	कदाचित् वह कल सभा में आये।	Kadāchit vah kal sabhā meṅ āye.
9. Lest he may escape away.	ऐसा न हो कहीं वह भाग जाये।	Aisā na ho, kahin vah bhāg jāye.
10. You may get admission either in science or in commerce.	या तुम विज्ञान में प्रवेश लो या वाणिज्य में।	Yā tum vigyān meṅ pravesh lo yā vāṇjiya meṅ.

25TH STEP पचीसवीं सीढ़ी

PAST TENSE (1)
भूतकाल (1)

1. *Past Indefinite* सामान्य भूत

1.	The students reached the classroom.	छात्र कक्षा में पहुंचे।	Chātra kaksā meiṅ puhuṅche.
2.	The police arrested the accused.	पुलिस ने अपराधी को गिरफ्तार किया।	Pulis ne aprādhi ko griftār kiyā.
3.	I saw him yesterday.	मैंने उसे कल देखा।	Maiṅ ne use kal dekhā.
4.	We sat down on the path while walking.	हम चलते-चलते राह पर बैठ गए।	Ham chalte-chalte rah par baiṭh gaye.
5.	I went to your house in the morning	मैं प्रात:काल तुम्हारे घर गया।	Main prāta:kāl tumhare ghar gayā.
6.	We gave her a warm welcome.	हमने उस (महिला) का हार्दिक स्वागत किया।	Ham ne us (mahilā) ka hārdik swāgat kiyā.

7. The teacher punished the naughty students.	अध्यापक ने शरारती छात्रों को दण्ड दिया।	Adhyapak ne shararti chatron ko dand diya.
8. You witnessed the match.	तुमने मैच देखा।	Tum ne maich dekhā.
9. The children ran and played.	बच्चे भागे और खेले।	Bachche bhāge aur khele.
10. They laughed at the begger.	वे भिखारी पर हँसे।	Ve bhikhāri par haṅse.
11. The girls sang a song.	लड़कियों ने गीत गाया।	Laṛkion ne git gāyā.
12. The mother told a story of king.	मां ने राजा की एक कहानी कही।	Maṅ ne rajā ki ek kahāni kahi.
13. The baby took a sound sleep.	बच्चा गहरी नींद सोया।	Bachcha gahri niṅd soyā.
14. Rekha wrote a letter to her fast friend.	रेखा ने अपनी पक्की सहेली को पत्र लिखा।	Rekhā ne apni pakki saheli ko patra likhā.
15. They ate, drank and became happy.	उन्होंने खाया-पिया और प्रसन्न हुए।	Unhoṅne khāyā, piyā aur prasanna hue.

2. *Presnet Perfect* आसन्न भूत

1. I have done my work.	मैं अपना काम कर चुका हूं।	Main apnā kām kar chukā hūṅ.
2. She has seen me in the restaurant.	वह मुझे रेस्तरां में देख चुकी है।	Vah mujhe restarāṅ me dekh chuki hai.
3. You have read this book.	आपने यह पुस्तक पढ़ी है।	Apne-yah pustak paṛhi hai.

4.	I have finished my work.	मैं अपना काम पूरा कर चुकी हूँ।	Maiṅ apnā kām pūrā kar chuki hūṅ.
5.	My mother has arrived at home.	मेरी माताजी घर पहुंच चुकी हैं।	Meri matāji ghar pahuṅch chuki hain.
6.	Garima has sung a song.	गरिमा ने गीत गाया है।	Garimā ne git gaya hai.
7.	The students have gone to their home.	छात्र अपने घरों को जा चुके हैं।	Chātra apne gharoṅ ko jā chuke hain.
8.	The sweeper has just washed the floor.	जमादार ने अभी-अभी फर्श साफ किया है।	Jamadār ne abhi abhi farsh sāf kiyā hai.
9.	The phone has stopped ringing.	फोन बजना बंद हो गया है।	Phon bajna band ho gayā hai.
10.	Someone has broken the clock.	किसी ने दीवाल-घड़ी तोड़ दी है।	Kisine diwāl-ghari tor di hai.
11.	They have heard the sad news.	वे दुःखद समाचार सुन चुके हैं।	Ve du:khad samāchār sun chuke hain
12.	She has made the coffee.	उसने कॉफी बनाई है।	Usne kāfi banāi hai.
13.	I have paid the bill.	मैंने बिल चुका दिया है।	Maiṅ ne bill chuka diyā hai.
14.	Father has planted a tree.	पिताजी ने पेड़ लगाया है।	Pitāji ne per lagāyā hai.
15.	The play has just began.	नाटक अभी शुरू हुआ है।	Nātāk abhi shurū huā hai.

3. *Past Perfect* पूर्ण भूत

1.	I had already written the letter.	मैं पहले से ही पत्र लिख चुका था।	Maiṅ pahle se hi patra likh chukā tha.
2.	She had seen this picture before.	वह इस फिल्म को पहले देख चुकी थी।	Vah is film ko pahle dekh cuki thi.
3.	Till last evening I had not seen him.	कल सायंकाल तक मैंने उसे नहीं देखा था।	Kal sāyankāl tak maiṅe use nahin dekhā thā.
4.	Anil had gone home before Amit came.	अमित के आने से पहले अनिल घर जा चुका था।	Amit ke āne se pahle Anil ghar jā chukā thā.
5.	I had finished my breakfast when Rita came.	जब रीता आई मैं नाश्ता कर चुका था।	Jab Ritā āyi maiṅ nashtā kar chukā thā.
6.	We had lived in Lajpat Nagar since 1950.	हम 1950 से लाजपत नगर में रह रहे थे।	Ham 1950 se Lājpat Nagar meiṅ rah rahe they.
7.	I had waited for you for the last five days.	मैं पिछले पांच दिनों से तुम्हारा इंतजार कर रहा था।	Maiṅ pichle pāṅch dinoṅ se tumhāra intzār kar rahā thā.
8.	We had never seen such a match before.	हमने ऐसा मैच पहले कभी नहीं देखा था।	Hamne aisā maich pahle kabhi nahin dekhā thā.
9.	She had drunk the water.	वह पानी पी चुकी थी।	Vah pāni pi chuki thi.
10.	My sister had passed the degree examination.	मेरी बहन डिग्री की परीक्षा पास कर चुकी थी।	Meri bahin Digri ki paṛiksā pās kar chuki thi.

11.	I had come here to meet you.	मैं यहां तुम्हें मिलने आया था।	Maiṅ yahāṅ tumheṅ milne āyā tha.
12.	They had not paid the debt.	उन्होंने उधार नहीं चुकाया था।	Unhoṅne udhār nahiṅ chukāyā thā.
13.	We had purhased the shirts.	हमने कमीजें खरीदी थीं।	Ham ne kamijeṅ kharidiṅ thiṅ.
14.	The train had left the platform when we reached.	हमारे पहुंचने से पहले गाड़ी प्लेटफार्म छोड़ चुकी थी।	Hamāre pahunchne se pahle gārī platform chhor chuki thi.
15.	He had seen this picture.	वह यह फिल्म देख चुका था।	Vah yah film dekh chukā thā.

26TH STEP छब्बीसवीं सीढ़ी

PAST TENSE (2)
भूत काल (2)

4. *Doubtful Past* संदिग्ध भूत

1. Yashodharā might have come.	यशोधरा आयी होगी।	Yashodharā āyī hogi.
2. You might have heard the name of Tagore.	तुमने टैगोर का नाम अवश्य सुना होगा।	Tumne Tagor kā nām avashya sunā hoga.
3. She might have forgotten the past.	वह अपना बीता समय भूल गई होगी।	Vah apnā bitā samay bhūl gai hogi.
4. They might have slept.	वे सो गए होंगे।	Ve so gaya hoṅge.
5. They might have paid her the old dues.	उन्होंने पुरानी देनदारी उसे चुका दी होगी।	Unhoṅ ne purāni dendāri use chūkā di hogi.
6. He might have thought that I would be still there.	उसने सोचा होगा कि मैं वहीं हूं।	Usne sochā hogā ki main vahiṅ hūṅ.

7.	Mr. Malik might have written the letter.	श्री मलिक ने पत्र लिखा होगा।	Shri Malik ne patra likhā hogā.
8.	The institution might have invited the Mayor.	संस्थान ने मेयर को निमंत्रित किया होगा।	Sansthān ne meyar ko nimaṅtrit kiyā hogā.
9.	They might have laughed when she begged.	वे हंसे होंगे जब उसने भीख मांगी होगी।	Ve hanse hoṅge jab usne bhikh māngi hogi.
10.	They might have accepted it.	उन्होंने इसे स्वीकार कर लिया होगा।	Unhoṅ ne ise swikār kar liyā hogā.
11.	She might have done her duty.	उसने अपना कर्त्तव्य पूरा किया होगा।	Usne apnā kartavya pura kiyā hogā.
12.	The author might have written his auto-biography.	लेखक ने अपनी आत्मकथा लिखी होगी।	Lekhak ne apni atmakathā likhi hogi.

5. *Past Imperfect* अपूर्ण भूत

1.	I was writing a letter when he entered the room.	मैं पत्र लिख रहा था जब वह कमरे में घुसा।	Maiṅ patra likh rahā thā jab vah kamre meṅ ghusā.
2.	I was riding to school yesterday.	कल मैं घोड़े पर बैठकर स्कूल जा रहा था।	Kal maiṅ ghoṛe par baiṭh kar skūl jā rahā thā.
3.	It was raining when I went out.	जब मैं बाहर गया तो बारिश हो रही थी।	Jab maiṅ bāhar gayā to bārish ho rahi thi.

4. While I was talking to her I heard a shout.	जब मैं उससे बात कर रहा था तो मैंने एक चीख सुनी।	Jab maiṅ usse bāt kar rahā thā to maiṅ ne ek chikh suni.
5. He was writing an essay in Hindi.	वह हिंदी में निबंध लिख रहा था।	Vah Hinai meiṅ nibaṅdh likh rahā thā.
6. When they were sleeping the dogs were watching.	जब वे सो रहे थे तो कुत्ते पहरा दे रहे थे।	Jab ve so rahe the to kutte pahrā de rahe they.
7. We were playing tennis when your brother came.	जब तुम्हारा भाई आया तो हम टेनिस खेल रहे थे।	Jab tumhārā bhāi ayā to ham tenis khel rahe they.
8. Reena was trying hard to hide her desire.	रीना अपनी इच्छा को छिपाने की कोशिश कर रही थी।	Rinā apni iccha ko chipāne ki barī koshish kar rahi thi.
9. They were talking too loudly in the meeting.	वे गोष्ठी में बहुत तेज बोल रहे थे।	Ve gosṭhi meṅ bahut tez bol rahe they.
10. Asha was studying with me in the school.	आशा मेरे साथ स्कूल में पढ़ रही थी।	Āshā mere sāth skūl meṅ paṛh rahi thi.

There is a slight difference between रहा था/रही थी and –ता था/–ती थी। The former shows merely the continuity of the action in the period indicated, the latter expresses an idea of habit or repeated action.

Here are some sentences have ता था/ती थी, etc. These also the example of अपूर्ण भूत Apurna Bhut.

11. We were living	दो वर्ष पहले हम	Do varṣe pahle ham

	in Pune two years ago.	पुणे में रहते थे।	Puṇe men rahte the.
12.	Formerly this cow was giving ten litre of milk.	पहले यह गाय दस कीलोलीटर दूध देती थी।	Pahle yah gāy das litar dūdh deti thi.
13.	In the last world war, the Germans were fighting bravely.	गत विश्वयुद्ध में जर्मन बड़ी वीरता से लड़ते थे।	Gaṭ vishva yudhha meiṅ Jarman bari virtā se laṛte the.
14.	At that time, I was residing in Delhi.	उस समय मैं दिल्ली में निवास करता था।	Us samay maiṅ Dilli meṅ nivās kartā thā.
15.	I used to go daily to the temple.	मैं प्रतिदिन मंदिर जाता था।	Maiṅ prātidin mandir jātā tha.
16.	Before 1947 we were living in West Panjab.	1947 से पूर्व हम पश्चिमी पंजाब में रहते थे।	1947 se pūrva ham paschimi Panjāb meiṅ rahte the.
17.	When I was seven years old, I was going to school all alone.	जब मैं सात वर्ष का था मैं अकेला स्कूल जाता था।	Jab maiṅ sat varṣa kā thā, main akelā skūl jātā thā.
18.	In my early age, my granmother was telling the story to me.	जब मैं छोटी थी, मेरी दादी मां मुझे कहानी सुनाया करती थी।	Jab maiṅ chhoti thi, meri dādi māṅ mujhe kahāni sunāyā karti thi.
19.	In his seventy he used to walk very fast.	सत्तर साल की आयु में बहुत तेज चलता था।	Sattar sāl ki āyū meṅ vah bahut tez chaltā thā.

6. *Past Conditional* हेतु हेतु मद् भूत

1. If you had worked hard, you would have passed.	यदि तुम परिश्रम करते तो उत्तीर्ण हो जाते।	Yadi tūm parishram karte to uttirṇa ho jāte.
2. Had you been honest you would have been happier.	यदि तुम ईमानदार होते तो तुम अधिक सुखी होते।	Yadi tūm imāndār hote to tūm adhik sukhi hote.
3. If she had been clever she would have not done so.	यदि वह बुद्धिमती होती तो वह ऐसा न करती।	Yadi vah budhimati hoti to vah aisa nā karti.
4. Had you sung, we would have enjoyed.	यदि तुमने गाया होता तो हम आनंद लेते।	Yadi tūm ne gāyā hotā to ham ānand lete.
5. If she had reached I would have gone.	यदि वह पहुंची होती तो मैं चला जाता।	Yadi vah pahuṅchi hoti to maiṅ chalā jātā.
6. Had you came I would have played.	यदि तुम आए होते तो मैं खेलता।	Yadi tūm āye hote to maiṅ kheltā.
7. If you had written to me I would have replied to you.	यदि तुमने मुझे लिखा होता मैं तुम्हें उत्तर देता।	Yadi tūm ne likhā hotā to maiṅ tumheṅ uttar detā.
8. Have you asked me I would have stayed?	यदि तुमने मुझे कहा होता तो मैं रह जाता।	Yadi tūm ne mujhe kahā hotā to maiṅ rah jātā.

9.	If she had told me earlier I would have not done so.	यदि उसने मुझे पहले बताया होता तो मैं ऐसा न करता।	Yadi usne mujhe pahle batāyā hotā to maiṅ aisā na kartā.
10.	Had you invited her she would have come.	यदि तुम उसे निमंत्रित करते तो वह जरूर आती।	Yadi tūm use nimaṅtrit karte to vaḥ zarūr āti.
11.	Had Radha wings she would have flown over to Krishna.	यदि राधा के पंख होते तो वह उड़कर कृष्ण के पास पहुँच जाती।	Yadi Rādhā ke paṅkh hote to vah urkar Krishna ke pas pahuṅch jāti.
12.	It she had liked the camera she would have bought it.	यदि उसे कैमरा पसंद होता तो उसने उसे खरीद लिया होता।	Yadi use kaimrā pasand hota to usne use kharid liyā hotā.

27TH STEP सत्ताईसवीं सीढ़ी

INTERROGATIVE SENTENCES (1)
प्रश्नसूचक वाक्य (1)

Interrogative Sentences with

(1) IS ARE AM WAS WERE

है हो/हैं हूं था/थी थे/थीं

1. Is Hindi difficult?	क्या हिंदी कठिन है?	Kyā Hindi kathin hai?
2. Is it cold today?	आज ठण्ड है?	Aj ṭhanḍ hai?
3. Is your name Narendra Kumar?	आपका नाम नरेन्द्र कुमार है?	Āpkā nām Narendra Kumār hai?
4. Are you afraid of ghost?	तुम भूतों से डरते हो?	Tum bhūtoṅ se ḍarte ho?
5. Are you feeling well?	तुम स्वस्थ हो?	Tum swastha ho?
6. Are you Mr. Amitabh.	तुम श्री अमिताभ हो?	Tum Shri Amitabh ho?
7. Am I afraid of you?	मैं तुमसे डरता हूं?	Maiṅ tum se ḍartā hūṅ?

8. Am I a fool?	मैं मूर्ख हूं?	Maiṅ mūrkha hūṅ?
9. Am I your servant?	मैं तुम्हारा नौकर हूं?	Maiṅ tumhārā naukar huṅ?
10. Was she frightened?	वह डरी हुई थी?	Vah ḍari hūi thi?
11. Was he a stranger here?	वह यहां अजनबी है?	Vah yahāṅ ajnabi hai?
12. Was the moon shining?	चांद चमक रहा था?	Chāṅd chamak rahā thā?
13. Were the boys playing football?	लड़के फुटबाल खेल रहे थे?	Laṛke fūtbal khel rahe the?
14. Were you enjoying yourself in Simla?	तुम शिमला में आनंद से रहे?	Tum Shimlā meṅ anand se rahe?
15. Were you not happy with your collegues?	क्या तुम अपने साथियों के साथ प्रसन्न नहीं थे?	Kyā tūm apne sāthioṅ ke sāth prasanna nahiṅ the?

(2) ḌO, DOES, DID

ता, ते, ती

16. Do we shirk work?	क्या हम काम से जी चुराते हैं?	Kyā ham kām se ji churāte haiṅ?
17. Do you smoke?	आप धूम्रपान करते हैं?	Āp dūmrapān karte haiṅ?
18. Do you always speak the truth?	तुम सदा सच बोलते हो?	Tum sadā sach bolte ho?
19. Does she like to dress well?	वह अच्छी वेशभूषा पसंद करती है?	Vah achchhi veshbūṣa pasand karti hai?
20. Does he play games?	वह खेल खेलता है?	Vah khel kheltā hai?

21. Does she like her neighbour?	वह अपने पड़ोसी को पसंद करती है?	Vah apne pṛosi ko pasand karti hai?
22. Did Anupam eat all the apples?	अनुपम ने सभी सेब खा लिये?	Anupam ne sabhi seb khā liye?
23. Did yo build it?	तुमने इसे बनाया?	Tum ne ise banāyā?
24. Did you ring the bell?	क्या तुमने घण्टी बजायी?	Kyā tum ne ghaṅti bajayi?

(3) HAS, HAVE, HAD

चुका है, चुकी है

25. Has he written to father?	क्या उसने पिता को लिखा है?	Kyā usne pitā ko likhā hai?
26. Has her temperature gone down?	क्या उसका तापमान गिर गया है?	Kyā Us ka tāpmān gir gayā hai?
27. Has Anurag missed the train?	अनुराग से गाड़ी छुट गयी है?	Anurāg se gaṛi chhūṭ gayi hai?
28. Have you spent all your money?	तुमने अपना सारा धन खर्च कर दिया है क्या?	Tum ne apnā sārā dhan kharch kar diyā hai kyā?
29. Have you ever driven any car?	आपने कभी कोई कार चलायी है?	Āpne kabhi koi kār chalāyi hai?
30. Have you found my handkerchief?	तुम्हें मेरा रूमाल मिला है?	Tumheṅ merā rūmāl milā hai?
31. Had the postman delivered any letter?	क्या डाकिये ने कोई पत्र दिया था?	Kyā ḍākiye ne koi patra diyā thā?
32. Had you finished your work?	तुमने अपना काम पूरा कर लिया था?	Tum ne apnā kām pūrā kar liyā thā?

33.	Had you ever been to Bombay?	तुम कभी बम्बई गए थे?	Tum kabhi Bambai gaye the?

(4) WILL, SHALL, WOULD, SHOULD

-गा/गे -गा

34.	Will they attend the meeting in time?	क्या वे समय पर गोष्ठी में उपस्थित होंगे?	Kyā ve samay par gos̤ṭhi meiṅ upasṭhit hoṅge?
35.	Will you meet her at the station?	तुम उसे स्टेशन पर मिलोगे क्या?	Tum use steshan par miloge kyā?
36.	Shall I not apologize for my mistake?	क्या मुझे अपनी गलती के लिए क्षमा नहीं मांगनी होगी?	Kyā mujhe apni galti ke liya kṣamā nāhiṅ māṅgani chāhiya?
37.	Shall we call on her?	हमें उससे मिलना चाहिये क्या?	Hameṅ us se milnā chāhiya kyā?
38.	Would he give me some rupees if I needed?	यदि मुझे जरूरत हुई तो क्या वह कुछ रुपये दे देगा?	Yadi mujhe zarūrat hui to kyā vah kuchh rupaye de degā?
39.	Would you tell me the correct answer if I mistaken?	यदि मुझसे गलती हो गयी तो क्या तुम मुझे ठीक उत्तर बता दोगे?	Yadi mujhe se galti ho gai to kyā tūm mujhe ṭhik uttar batā doge?
40.	Should I not distub you?	क्या मुझे आपको बाधा नहीं पहुंचानी चाहिए?	Kya mujhe āpko bādhā nahiṅ pahuṅchāni chāhiye?
41.	Should we forget noble acts of others?	क्या हमें दूसरों के अच्छे कार्यों को भूल जाना चाहिए?	Kyā hameṅ dūsroṅ ke achchhe kāryoṅ ko bhṅl jānā chāhiye?

(5) CAN, COULD, MAY

सकना, सकते, सके

42.	Can you solve this riddle?	क्या तुम इस पहेली को हल कर सकते हो?	Kyā tūm is paheli ko hal kar ṣakte ho?
43.	Can you jump over this fence?	क्या तुम इस जंगले को फांद सकते हो?	Kyā tṅm is jangle ko phāṅd ṣakte ho?
44.	Could he come in time?	क्या वह समय पर आ सका?	Kyā vah samay par ā sakā?
45.	Could we do this job alone?	क्या हम यह काम अकेले कर सके?	Kyā hum yah kām akele kar sake?
46.	May I come in, Sir?	क्या मैं अंदर आ सकती हूं, श्रीमान?	Kyā maiṅ āndar ā sakti hūṅ, Shrimān?
47.	May I accompany you, Madam?	क्या मैं आपका साथ दे सकता हूं, श्रीमती?	Kyā maiṅ āpkā sāth de saktā hūṅ, Shrimati?
48.	May I have your attention?	क्या मैं आपका ध्यान आकृष्ट कर सकता हूँ?	Kyā maiṅ āpkā dhyān akriṣṭ kar saktā hūṅ?

28TH STEP अट्ठाईसवीं सीढ़ी

INTERROGATIVE SENTENCES (2)
प्रश्नसूचक वाक्य (2)

Interrogative Sentences With

(1) WHAT WHEN WHERE WHY
क्या कब कहां क्यों

1.	What is your name?	तुम्हारा क्या नाम है?	Tumhārā kyā nām hai?
2.	What is your age?	तुम्हारी कितनी उम्र है?	Tumhāri kitni umra hai?
3.	What does this mean?	इसका क्या अभिप्राय है?	Iskā kyā abhiprāy hai?
4.	What do you want?	तुम क्या चाहते हो?	Tum kyā chāhte ho?
5.	What did you pay?	आपने कितना (मूल्य) चुकाया?	Āpne kitnā (mūlya) chukāyā?
6.	What will you take?	आप क्या लेंगे?	Āp kyā lenge?
7.	What o'clock is it?	इस समय कितने बजे हैं?	Is samay kitne baje haiṅ?

8. What colour do you like?	आप कौन सा रंग पसंद करते हैं?	Āp kaunsā raṅg pasaṅd karte haiṅ?
9. What wages do you want?	तुम कितनी मजदूरी चाहते हो?	Tum kitni mazdūri chahte ho?
10. What is your hobby?	आपकी क्या अभिरुचि है?	Āpki kyā abhirūchi haiṅ?
11. When do you get up in the morning?	आप सुबह कब उठते हैं?	Āp subah kab uṭhte haiṅ?
12. When did you hear this news?	तुमने यह समाचार कब सुना?	Tumne yah samāchār kab sunā?
13. When shall we retern?	हम कब लौटेंगे?	Ham kab lauteṅge?
14. When will you finish your work?	तुम अपना काम कब समाप्त करोगे?	Tum apnā kām kab samāpta karoge?
15. When did she tell you her story?	उसने तुम्हें अपनी कहानी कब सुनायी?	Usne tumheṅ apni kahāni kab sunāyi?
16. When will they meet again?	वे दुबारा अब कब मिलेंगे?	Ve dubārā ab kab mileṅge?
17. When was your car stolen?	तुम्हारी कार कब चोरी हुई?	Tumhāri kār kab chori hui?
18. When do you wear your new clothes?	तुम अपने नये कपड़े कब पहनते हो?	Tum apne naye kapṛe kab pahante ho?
19. When do we have to leave this station?	हमें इस स्टेशन को कब छोड़ना पड़ेगा?	Hameṅ is steshan ko kab chhoṛnā paṛegā?

20.	When did you sleep at night?	तुम रात को कब सोते हो?	Tum rāt ko kab sote ho?
21.	Where is your purse?	तुम्हारा बटुआ कहां है?	Tumhārā baṭuā kahāṅ hai?
22.	Where are you going?	आप कहां जा रहे हैं?	Āp kahāṅ jā rahe haiṅ?
23.	Where do they live?	वे कहां रहते हैं?	Ve kahāṅ rahte haiṅ?
24.	Where does this path lead do?	यह रास्ता किधर जाता है?	Yah rāṣtā kidhar jātā hai?
25.	Where have you come from?	आप कहां से आये हैं?	Āp kahāṅ se āye haiṅ?
26.	Where can we obtain books?	हम पुस्तकें कहां से प्राप्त कर सकते हैं?	Ham pustkeṅ kahāṅ se pṛapta kar sakte haiṅ?
27.	Where was your watch made?	आपकी घड़ी कहां की बनी है?	Āpki ghaṛi kahaṅ ki bani hai?
28.	Where do you buy tea?	तुम चाय कहां से खरीदते हो?	Tum chāy kahāṅ se kharidte ho?
29.	Where can I get down	मैं कहां उतर सकता हूं?	Main kahāṅ utar saktā hūṅ?
30.	Where shall we go now?	अब हम कहां जायेंगे?	Ab ham kahāṅ jāyeṅge?
31.	Why does he not apply for this post?	वह इस पद के लिए प्रार्थना-पत्र क्यों नहीं देता?	Vah iś pad ke liye prārthanā-patra kyoṅ nahiṅ detā.
32.	Why do you not come early?	तुम जल्दी क्यों नहीं आये?	Tum jaldi kyoṅ nahiṅ āye?

33. Why did she abuse me?	उसने मुझे गाली क्यों दी?	Usne mujhe gālī kyoṅ di?
34. Why do you drink so much?	आप इतनी (शराब) क्यों पीते हैं?	Āp itni (sharab) kyoṅ pite haiṅ?
35. Why do you not solve my querries?	आप मेरे प्रश्नों का समाधान क्यों नहीं करते हैं?	Āp mere prashnoṅ kā samādhān kyoṅ nahiṅ karte haiṅ?
36. Why are you so sad today?	आज आप इतने उदास क्यों हैं?	Āj āp itne udās kyoṅ haiṅ?
37. Why was your mother angry with you?	तुम्हारी माता जी तुमसे नाराज क्यों थी?	Tumhāri mātāji tum se nārāz kyoṅ thi?
38. Why do some people travel abroad?	कुछ लोग विदेश यात्रा क्यों करते हैं?	Kuchh log videsh yātrā kyoṅ karte haiṅ?
39. Why was that M.L.A. sent to prison?	उस एम. एल. ए. को जेल क्यों भेजा गया?	Us em.el.a. ko jel kyoṅ bhejā gayā?
40. Why do you not try to understand me?	आप मुझे समझने की कोशिश क्यों नहीं करते?	Āp mujhe samajhne ki koshish kyoṅ nahiṅ karte?

(2) WHO WHOM WHOSE

कौन किसको किसका

41. Who is that fellow?	वह व्यक्ति कौन है?	Vah vyakti kaun hai?
42. Who lives in this house?	इस घर में कौन रहता है?	Is ghar meṅ kaun rahtā hai?

43.	Who sang this song?	यह गीत किसने गाया?	Yah git kisne gāyā?
44.	Who repairs the watches?	घड़ियां कौन ठीक करता है?	Ghariāṅ kaun ṭhik kartā hai?
45.	Who controlled the traffic?	यातायात नियंत्रण कौन करता है?	Yātāyāt niyaṅtraṇ kaun kartā hai?
46.	Whom do you want?	आप किसे चाहते हैं?	Āp kise chāhte haiṅ?
47.	By whom are you employed?	आप किसके द्वारा नौकरी पर रखे गए हैं?	Āp kiske dwārā naukari par rakhe gaye haiṅ?
48.	Whom had you promised?	आपने किसे वचन दिया है?	Āpne kise vachan diyā hai?
49.	Whose house is that?	वह मकान किसका है?	Vah makān kiskā hai?
50.	In whose employment are our teachers?	हमारे अध्यापक किसकी नौकरी में हैं?	Hamāre adhyāpak kiski naukari meṅ haiṅ?

29TH STEP उन्नीतीसवीं सीढ़ी

INTERROGATIVE SENTENCES (3)
प्रश्नसूचक वाक्य (3)

Interrogative Sentences with

(3) HOW HOW LONG HOW MANY HOW MUCH

कैसे कब तक/कहां तक कितने कितना

1.	How do you do?	आपका क्या हालचाल है?	Āpkā kyā hālchāl hai?
2.	How do you feel now?	अब आप कैसे हैं?	Ab āp kaise haiṅ?
3.	How do you come to know the truth?	आपको सच्चाई का कैसे पता चला?	Āpko sachchāi ka kaise patā chalā?
4.	How are you?	आप कैसे हैं?	Āp kaise haiṅ?
5.	How old are you?	आपकी उम्र क्या है?	Āpki umra kyā hai?
6.	How is it possible?	यह कैसे संभव है?	Yah kaise sambhav hai?
7.	How old is your son?	आपका लड़का कितना बड़ा है?	Āpkā laṛkā kitnā baṛā hai?

8. How do you manage it?	आपने इसका प्रबंध कैसे किया?	Āpne iskā prabaṅdh kaise kiyā?
9. How long have you been in India.	आप भारत में कितने समय से हैं?	Āp Bhārat meiṅ kitne samay se haiṅ?
10. How long has your mother been sick?	आपकी माताजी कितने समय से बीमार है?	Āpki matāji kitne samay se bimār haiṅ?
11. How long do they want the rooms for?	वे कितने समय के लिए कमरे चाहते हैं?	Ve kitne samay ke liye kamre chāhte haiṅ?
12. How long is post-office from your residence?	आपके घर से डाकखाना कितनी दूर है?	Āpke ghar se dāk-khana kitni dūr hai?
13. How long is this room?	यह कमरा कितना लम्बा है?	Yah kamrā kitnā lambā hai?
14. How long is the capital from here?	यहां से राजधानी कितनी दूरी पर है?	Yahāṅ se rājdhāni kitni dūri par hai?
15. How many family members have you?	आपके कुटुम्ब में कितने व्यक्ति हैं?	Āpke kuṭumb meṅ kitne vyakti haiṅ?
16. How many brothers and sisters are you?	आपके कितने भाई-बहन हैं?	Āpke kitne bhāi-bahin haiṅ?
17. How many seats are there in the bus?	बस में कितनी सीटें हैं?	Bas meṅ kitni siṭeṅ haiṅ?
18. How much	कितनी राशि देनी	Kitni rāshi deni

	money is to be paid?	है?	hai?
19.	How much do you charge per head?	प्रति व्यक्ति आप क्या लेंगे?	Prati vyakti āp kyā leṅge?
20.	How much milk is required?	कितना दूध चाहिए?	Kitnā dūdh chāhiye?

(4) WHICH

कौन सा/कौन सी

21.	Which is your umbrella?	तुम्हारी छतरी कौन सी है?	Tumhāri chhatri kaun si hai?
22.	Which picture will you see on Sunday?	तुम रविवार को कौन सी फिल्म देखोगे?	Tum Ravivār ko kaunsi film dekhoge?
23.	Which is the right way?	कौन सा रास्ता ठीक है?	Kaun sā rāstā ṭhik hai?
24.	Which is the booking office?	टिकट-घर कौन सा है?	Tikaṭ-ghar kaun sā hai?
25.	Which is your favourite book?	तुम्हारी मन-पसंद पुस्तक कौन सी है?	Tumhāri man-pasand pustak kaunsi hai?
26.	From which platform the frontier mail arrive?	किस प्लेटफॉर्म पर फ्रांटियर मेल आएगी?	Kis plaiṭform par fronṭiar mel āyegī?

30TH STEP तीसवीं सीढ़ी

NEGATIVE SENTENCES
निषेधसूचक वाक्य

Interrogative Sentences with

(1) NOT NO-NOT NO NEVER NOTHING SELDOM
नहीं न-नहीं न कदापि नहीं नहीं कभी नहीं

1. My father is not feeling well.	मेरे पिताजी की तबियत ठीक नहीं है।	Mere pitāji ki tabiyat ṭhik nahiṅ hai?
2. We are not fool.	हम मूर्ख नहीं हैं।	Hum mūrkha nahiṅ haiṅ.
3. I don't know what you say.	मैं नहीं जानती आपने क्या कहा।	Maiṅ nahiṅ janti āpne kyā kahā.
4. I don't know who she is.	मैं नहीं जानता वह कौन है।	Maiṅ nahiṅ jāntā vah kaun hai.
5. No, I don't understand.	नहीं, मैं नहीं समझा।	Nahiṅ, maiṅ nahiṅ samjhā.
6. I know nothing about it.	मैं इस बारे में कुछ नहीं जानता।	Maiṅ is bāre meiṅ kuchh nahiṅ jantā.
7. Nothing particular.	कोई बात नहीं।	koi bāt nahiṅ.
8. I did not want anything.	मैंने कुछ नहीं चाहा।	Maine kuchh nahiṅ chāhā.

9. No sir, the boss has not come yet.	नहीं श्रीमान्, साहब अभी नहीं आए हैं।	Nahiṅ shrimān, sāhāb abhi nahiṅ aye haiṅ.
10. No thorough fare.	आम रास्ता नहीं।	Am rāstā nahiṅ.
11. No, I have headache.	नहीं, मुझे सिरदर्द है।	Nahiṅ, mujhe ṣirdard hai.
12. No, not at all, She is not trustworthy.	नहीं, बिल्कुल नहीं। वह विश्वासपात्र नहीं है।	Nahiṅ, bilkul nahiṅ Vah vishwāspātra nahiṅ hai.
13. Barking dogs seldom bite.	भौंकते हुए कुत्ते कभी नहीं काटते। (जो गरजते हैं वे बरसते नहीं)	Bhauṅkte hue kutte kabhi nahiṅ kāṭate.
14. One has never seen such as absurd man.	किसी ने ऐसा असभ्य व्यक्ति नहीं देखा है।	Kisine aisā asabhya vyakti nahiṅ dekhā hai.
15. Do not touch it	इसे मत छुओ।	Ise mat chhuo.

(2) Negative Sentences with Interrogation

प्रश्न-सहित निषेधसूचक वाक्य

16. I can jump. Can't I?	मैं कूद सकता हूं। क्या नहीं?	Maiṅ kūd saktā huṅ. Kyā nahiṅ?
17. We shall return in time. Shan't we?	हम समय पर लौट आएंगे। क्या नहीं?	Ham samay par lauṭ āyeṅge. Kyā nahiṅ?
18. They will surely come. Won't they?	वे अवश्य आयेंगे। क्या नहीं?	Ve avashya āyeṅge. Kyā nahiṅ?
19. They are fool. Aren't they?	वे मूर्ख हैं। क्या नहीं?	Ve mūrkha haiṅ. Kyā nahiṅ?

20. You should not abuse others. Should you?	तुम्हें दूसरों को गाली नहीं देनी चाहिए। देनी चाहिए?	Tumheṅ dūsroṅ ko gali nahiṅ deni chāhiye. Deni chāhiye?
21. You must not smoke. Must you?	तुम्हें सिगरेट बिल्कुल नहीं पीनी चाहिए। पीनी चाहिएघ	Tumheṅ sigret bilkul nahiṅ pini chāhiye. Pini chāhiye?
22. There is enough milk. Isn't it?	दूध काफी है। क्या नहीं?	Dudh kāfi hai. Kyā nahiṅ?
23. Can't you find your handkerchief?	क्या तुम अपना रूमाल नहीं ढूंढ़ सकते?	Kyā tum apna rūmal nahiṅ duṅḍh sakte?
24. Couldn't he have done better?	क्या वह इससे अच्छा काम नहीं कर सकता था?	Kyā vah isse achchhā kām nahiṅ kar saktā thā?
25. Won't you be able to come and see us?	क्या तुम हमें मिलने नहीं आ सकते थे?	Kyā tum hameṅ milne nahiṅ ā sakte the?
26. Aren't you going to walk now?	क्या तुम अब घूमने नहीं जा रहे हो?	Kyā tum ab ghūmne nahiṅ jā rahe ho?
27. Must not I tell you again?	क्या मुझे तुमको दुबारा नहीं बताना पड़ेगा।	Kya mujhe tum ko dubārā nahiṅ batānā paregā?
28. Don't I have to close the shop?	क्या मुझे दुकान बंद नहीं करनी पड़ेगी।	Kyā mujhe dukān band nahiṅ karni paregi?

PART 4
SITUATIONAL SENTENCES

31ST STEP इक्तीसवीं सीढ़ी

AT HOME
घर में

1. You visited after a long time.	आपने बड़े दिनों के बाद दर्शन दिए।	Āpne bare dinoṅ ke bād darshan diye?.
2. What brings you here?	आप कैसे पधारे?	Āp kaise padhāre?
3. What brings you here?	आपने कैसे कष्ट किया।	Āpne kaise kaṣṭa kiyā?
4. I seek your advice.	मुझे आपसे सलाह लेनी है।	Mujhe āpse salāh leni hai.
5. What is your opinion in this matter?	इस विषय में आपका क्या विचार है?	Is viṣay meiṅ apkā kyā vichār hai?
6. I have come for some important matter.	मैं किसी आवश्यक काम से आया हूं।	Maiṅ kiṣi āvashyak kām se āyā hūn.
7. She had some work with you.	उसे तुमसे एक काम था।	Use tumse ek kām thā.
8. Come some other time.	फिर कभी आना।	Phir kabhi ānā.

9. Both of you may come.	आप दोनों आना।	Āp donoṅ ānā.
10. Promise that you shall come.	वचन दो कि अवश्य आओगे।	Vachan do ki avashya āoge.
11. I don't remember your name.	मैं आपका नाम भूल गया हूं।	Maiṅ āpkā nām bhūl gayā hūṅ.
12. You are beyond recognition.	आप पहचाने नहीं जाते।	Āp pahchāne nahiṅ jāte.
13. I woke up early this morning.	आज प्रातः मेरी आंख जल्दी खुली।	Āj prātaḥ meri āṅkh jaldi khuli.
14. I did not think it proper to wake you up.	मैंने आपको जगाना उचित नहीं समझा।	Maine āpko jagānā uchit nahiṅ samijhā.
15. Are you still awake?	आप अभी तक जाग रहे हैं क्या?	Āp abhi tak jāg rāhē haiṅ kyā?
16. I shall rest for a while.	मैं तनिक विश्राम कर लूं।	Maiṅ tanik vishrām kar lūṅ.
17. Let them rest.	उन्हें आराम करने दीजिए।	Unheṅ ārām karne dijiye.
18. I shall come some other time.	मैं फिर कभी आऊंगा।	Maiṅ phir kabhi āūṅgā.
19. I am feeling sleepy.	मुझे नींद आ रही है।	Mujhe niṅd ā rahi hai.
20. Go and take rest.	बस अब आराम करो।	Bas ab ārām karo.
21. I have got a sound sleep.	मुझे गहरी नींद आयी है।	Mujhe gahri niṅd āyi hai.

22. Please inform me of her arrival.	कृपया मुझे उसके आने की खबर दे दें।	Kripayā mujhe uske āne ki khabar de deṅ.
23. He left long before.	वह बहुत पहले चला गया है।	Vah bahut pahle chalā gayā hai.
24. Why did you not go?	आप क्यों नहीं गए?	Āp kyoṅ nahiṅ gāye?
25. I could not go because of some urgent work.	मैं किसी आवश्यक काम के कारण नहीं जा सका।	Maiṅ kisi āvashyak kām ke kāraṇ nahiṅ jā sakā.
26. Why did you not come day before yesterday.	आप परसों क्यों नहीं आए?	Āp parsoṇ kyoṇ nahiṅ āye?
27. There was an urgent piece of work.	एक जरूरी काम आ पड़ा था।	Ek zarūri kām ā paṛā thā.
28. I have been out since morning.	मैं सुबह का घर से निकला हूं।	Main subah kā ghar se niklā hūṅ.
29. They must be waiting for me at home.	वे घर पर मेरी प्रतीक्षा कर रहे होंगे।	Ve ghar par meri pratiksā kar rahe hoṅge.
30. I cannot stay any longer now.	मैं अब और नहीं रुक सकती।	Main ab aur nahiṅ ruk saktā.
31. Good bye, see you again.	अच्छा विदा, फिर मिलेंगे।	Achchā vidā, phir mileṅge.

32ND STEP बत्तीसवीं सीढ़ी

SHOPPING
खरीदारी

1. Where is Central Market?	सेन्ट्रल मार्केट कहां है?	Senṭral mārkeṭ kahāṅ hai?
2. I am going there, follow me.	मेरे साथ चलो, मैं वहीं जा रहा हूं।	Mere sāth chalo, maiṅ vahiṅ jā rahā hūṅ.
3. I want to purchase some clothes.	मैं कुछ कपड़े खरीदना चाहता हूं।	Maiṅ kuchh kapre kharidnā chāhtā hūṅ.
4. Which is the cheapest and best shop?	सस्ती और सबसे अच्छी दुकान कौन-सी है?	Sabse sasti aur sabse achchhi dukān kaun-si hai?
5. How much money have you?	आपके पास कितने रुपये हैं?	Āpke pās kitne rupaye haiṅ?
6. Don't spend more than income.	अपनी आय से अधिक खर्च न कीजिए।	Apni āy se adhik kharch na kijiye.
7. Is the price fixed?	क्या एक दाम है।	Kya ek dām hai?

8. State your minimum price.	कम से कम दाम बताइए।	Kam se kam dām bataiye.
9. Will you give it for seventy rupees?	क्या आप यह सत्तर रुपये में देंगे?	Kyā āp yah sattar rupaye meiṅ deṅge?
10. Count the money.	रुपये गिन लीजिए।	Rupaye gin lijiye.
11. Give me the balance.	बाकी पैसे दे दो।	Baki paise de do.
12. Do you sell socks?	आप जुराबें बेचते हैं क्या?	Āp jurāheṅ bechte haiṅ kyā?
13. Buy this one.	यह खरीद लीजिए।	Yah kharid lijiye.
14. Show me another variety.	मुझे और कोई किस्म दिखाओ।	Mujhe aur koi kisam dikhao.
15. I do not want this.	मुझे यह नहीं चाहिए।	Mujhe yah nahin chahiye.
16. Not so costly.	इतना कीमती नहीं।	Itnā kimti nahiṅ.
17. I do not want this colour.	मुझे इस रंग का नहीं चाहिए।	Mujhe is raṅg kā nahiṅ chāhiye.
18. It is faded.	इसका रंग उड़ा हुआ है।	Iska raṅg uṛā huā hai.
19. This is good.	यह अच्छा है।	Yah achchhā hai.
20. It is very dear.	यह बहुत महंगा है।	Yah bahut mahaṅgā hai.
21. Quite cheap.	बिल्कुल सस्ता।	Bilkul sasta.
22. Will it shrink?	क्या यह सिकुड़ेगा।	Kya yah sikuṛegā?
23. Can you recommend a good shop for shoes?	क्या आप जूतों की दुकान बतला सकते हैं?	Kyā āp jutoṅ ki dukān batlā sakte haiṅ?

24. Bata shoes are quite reliable.	बाटा के जूते विश्वास के योग्य हैं।	Bātā ke jute vishwās ke yogya haiṅ.
25. May we get it for you?	क्या हम आपके लिए मंगवा दें?	Kyā ham āpke liye maṅgwā deṅ?
26. Is the shop far away?	क्या वह दुकान दूर है?	Kya vah dukān dūr hai?
27. How much for a pair?	एक जोड़े की क्या कीमत है?	Ek joṛe ki kyā kimat hai?
28. Where is my bill?	मेरा बिल कहां है?	Merā bil kahāṅ hai?
29. Which is the payment counter?	भुगतान करने का काउंटर कौन सा है?	Bhugtān karne kā kauṇṭar kaun sā hai?
30. Please give me the maximum discount.	कृपया मुझे अधिकतम कमीशन दीजिए।	Kripayā mujhe adhiktam kamishan dijiye.
31. The error or omission will be adjusted.	भूल चूक सुधार ली जायेगी।	Bhūl chūk sudhār li jayegi.

33RD STEP तैंतीसवीं सीढ़ी

CRAFTSMEN
दस्तकार

(1) Cobbler मोची

1.	Have you ment my shoes?	तुमने मेरे जूते मरम्मत कर दिए हैं क्या?	Tumne ṃere jūte marammat kar diye haiṅ kyā?
2.	I want to get resoled these shoes.	मैं अपने जूतों पर सोल लगवाना चाहता हूं।	Main apne jutoṅ par sol legwana chāhtā hūṅ.
3.	What would you charge for resoling?	आप सोल लगाने का क्या लेते हैं?	Ap sol lagāne kā kya lete haiṅ?
4.	Don't use nails, stitch it.	कील मत लगाइए, सिलाई कीजिए।	Kil mat lagāiye, silāi kijiye.
5.	I need white laces.	मुझे सफेद तस्मे चाहिए।	Mujhe safed tasme chāhiye.

(2) Watch-maker घड़ीबाज़

6.	What is wrong with your watch?	आपकी घड़ी में क्या खराबी है?	Apki ghāri meiṅ kyā kharābi hai?

7. This watch gains eight minutes a day.	मेरी घड़ी आठ मिनट आगे हो जाती है।	Meri ghāri āṭh minaṭ āge ho jāti hai.
8. That watch loses six minutes in 24 hours.	वह घड़ी चौबीस घंटों में छह मिनट पीछे हो जाती है।	Vah gari chaubis ghanton meiṅ chhah minaṭ pichhe ho jāti hai.
9. Did you drop this watch?	क्या यह तुमसे गिर गई थी?	Kya yah tumse gir gaye thi?
10. The balance of this watch is broken.	इस घड़ी की सुई गिर गयी है।	Is ghaṛi ki sui gir gayi hai?

(3) Tailor दर्जी

11. Is there any good tailor's shop?	क्या यहाँ किसी अच्छे दर्जी की दुकान है।	Kya yahan kisi achchhe darzi ki dukān hai?
12. I want to have suit stitched.	मैं एक सूट सिलवाना चाहता हूं।	Maiṅ ek sūṭ silwānā chāhtā hūṅ.
13. Would you like losse fitting.	क्या आप ढीली फिटिंग पसंद करते हैं।	kya āp dhili fitiṅg pāsaṅd kartē haiṅ.
14. No, I would like tight fitting.	नहीं, मैं चुस्त फिटिंग पसंद करता हूँ।	Nahin, maiṅ chusta fiting pasand kartā hūṅ.
15. Is the shirt ready?	क्या कमीज़ सिल गयी?	Kya kamiz sil gayi?
16. Yes, I have only to iron it.	हाँ, केवल इस्तरी करना शेष है।	Hāṅ, kewal istari karnā sheṣ hai.

(4) Hair-dresser नाई

17. How long do I have to wait?	मुझे कितनी देर इंतजार करना पड़ेगा?	Mujhe kitni der intzar karnā paṛega?
18. What do you charge for a clean shave?	आप एक सफाचट्ट शेव का क्या लेते हैं?	Ap ek safāchaṭ shev ka kyā lete haiṅ?
19. Please sharpen the razor.	कृपया उस्तरा तेज़ कर लीजिए।	Kripayā ustarā tez kar lijiye.
20. Your razor is blunt.	तुम्हारा उस्तरा कुंद है।	Tumhārā ustarā kuṅd hai.
21. Cut my hair, but not too short.	मेरे बाल काटिए, पर बहुत छोटे नहीं।	Mere bāl kāṭiye, par bahut chhote nahiṅ.

(5) Grocer पंसारी

22. This is fair price shop.	यह उचित दर की दुकान है।	Yah uchit dar kee dukān hai.
23. 'Fixed price' and 'No credit these are our haiṅ.	'एक दाम' और 'उधार नहीं' ये हमारे उसूल हैं।	EK DĀM aur UDHĀR NAHIN- ye hamāre usūl motos.
24. We arrange home delivery.	हम घर पर सामान पहुंचा देते हैं।	Ham ghar par sāmān pahuṅchā dete haiṅ.
25. Please give me one kg. pure Desi Ghee.	कृपया मुझे 1 किलो देसी घी दीजिए।	Kripayā mujhe ek kilo desi ghi dijiye.
26. How much is bill?	कितने पैसे हुए?	Kitne paise hue?

(6) Dry Cleaner/Washermen ड्राईक्लीनर/धोबी

27. I must have these clothes within a week.	मुझे ये कपड़े एक सप्ताह में चाहिए।	Mujhe ye kapaṛe ek saptāh men chāhiye.
28. I want this suit dry cleaned.	मैं यह सूट ड्राइक्लीन कराना चाहता हूँ।	Maiṅ yah sūṭ ḍraiklin karānā chāhtā hūṅ.
29. This shirt is not properly washed.	यह कमीज ठीक से नहीं धुली है।	Yah kamiz ṭhik se nahiṅ dhuli hai.
30. These are silken clothes. Wash them carefully.	ये रेशमी कपड़े हैं। इन्हें सावधानी से धोना।	Ye reshmi kapṛe haiṅ. Inheṅ sāvdhāni se dhonā.
31. The trousers are badly ironed.	पैंटें ठीक से इस्तरी नहीं हुई हैं।	Peṅṭeṅ ṭhik se istari nahiṅ hui haiṅ.
32. You must take them back.	इन्हें वापिस ले जाओ।	Inhen vapis le jao.
33. Your charges are too much.	तुम अधिक पैसे लगाते हो।	Tum adhik paise lagāte ho.
34. Of course, we have a prompt service.	बेशक, हम काम भी समय पर करते हैं।	Beshak, ham kām bhi samay par karte haiṅ.

34TH STEP चौंतीसवीं सीढ़ी

FOODS & DRINKS
खाद्य एवं पेय

1.	I am feeling hungry.	मुझे भूख लग रही है।	Mujhe būkh lag rahi hai.
2.	Where can I get a good meal?	मुझे अच्छा खाना कहां मिल सकता है?	Mujhe achchhā khānā kahāṅ mil saktā hai.
3.	Come, let us take our food.	चलो खाना खायें।	Chalo khānā khāyeṅ.
4.	What will you have?	आप क्या खायेंगे?	Āp kyā khāyeṅge?
5.	Please give me the menu.	मुझे मीनू दीजिए।	Mujhe minū dijiye.
6.	Get the breakfast ready.	नाश्ता तैयार कीजिए।	Nāshtā tāiyār kijiye.
7.	Please have your food with us today.	आज आप हमारे साथ खाना खाइए।	Āj āp hamāre sāth khānā khāiye.
8.	Do you have a special diet?	क्या आपके पास कोई विशेष आहार है?	Kyā āpke pās koi visheṣ āhār hai?

9. Do you prefer sweet or salty dish?	आपको मीठी चीज पसंद है या नमकीन?	Āpko mithi chiz pasaṅd hai yā namkin?
10. Please give me Gujrati dishes.	मुझे गुजराती भोजन दीजिए।	Mujhe Gujrāti bhojan dijiye.
11. Please give me salt and pepper.	मुझे नमक और मिर्च दीजिए।	Mujhe namak aur mirch dijiye.
12. The mango is my favourite fruit.	आम मेरा प्रिय फल है।	Ām merā priya phal hai.
13. What would you like to prefer–Indian or Continental food?	आप क्या खाना पसंद करेंगे- देशी या विदेशी भोजन?	Āp kyā khānā pasaṅd kareṅge– deṣhi ya videshi bhojan.
14. Which drink would you like to have–Campa or Limca?	आप पेय कौन-सा पसंद करेंगे-कैम्पा या लिम्का?	Āp peya kaun sā pasaṅd kareṅge- Kaimpā yā Limka?
15. Please give me a cup of coffee.	मुझे एक कप कॉफी दीजिए।	Mujhe ek kap kafi dijiye.
16. Would you like to have whisky?	क्या आप शराब लेंगे?	Kyā āp sharāb leṅge?
17. No sir, I will drink beer.	नहीं श्रीमान्, मैं बियर पीऊंगा।	Nahiṅ shrimān, maiṅ biyar pioṅga.
18. Please give me a little more water.	थोड़ा पानी और दीजिए।	Thorā pāni aur dijiye.

19. I am vegetarian, I can not take non-vegetarian dish.	मैं शाकाहारी हूं, मैं मांसाहारी आहार नहीं खा सकता।	Maiṅ shākāhāri hūn, maiṅ māṅsāhārī āhār nahiṅ kha saktā.
20. Food has been served.	खाना परोस दिया गया है।	Khānā paros diyā gayā hai.
21. The food is quite tasty.	खाना बहुत स्वादिष्ट बना है।	Khānā bahut swādista banā hai.
22. You have eaten very little.	आपने तो कुछ खाया ही नहीं।	Āpne to kuchh khāyā hi nahiṅ.
23. Please give me some appetizer.	कोई क्षुधावर्धक पेय दीजिए।	Koi ksudhavardhak peya dijiye.
24. I have to go to a party.	मुझे एक दावत में जाना है।	Mujhe ek dāwat meṅ jānā hai.
25. Please bring some milk for me.	हमारे लिए कुछ दूध लाओ।	Hamare liye kuchh dūdh lāo.
26. Please put only a little sugar in the milk.	दूध में चीनी कम डालिए।	Dūdh meiṅ chini kam dāliye.
27. Please have this soft drink.	लो, शर्बत पीओ।	Lo, sharbat pio.
28. Have a little more.	थोड़ा और लीजिए।	Thoṛa aur lijiye.
29. Bring a cup of tea.	एक कप चाय लीजिए।	Ek kap chāy lijiye.

30. I don't like tea.	मुझे चाय अच्छी नहीं लगती।	Mujhe chāy achchhi nahin lagti.
31. Thanks, I am fully gratified.	धन्यवाद, मैं बड़ा तृप्त हो गया हूं।	Dhanyavād, maiṅ barā tripta ho gaya hūṅ.
32. Please give me the bill.	बिल लाइए।	Bil lāiye.
33. Is the service charges included?	क्या इसमें सेवा-राशि लगा दी गई है?	Kyā ismeṅ sevā-rāshi lagā di gai hai?
34. No sir, that is extra.	नहीं श्रीमान्, वह अलग है।	Nahiṅ shrimān! vah alag hai.
35. Please help me to wash my hunds.	मुझे हाथ धुलाइये।	Mujhe hāth dhulāiye.

35TH STEP पैंतीसवीं सीढ़ी

HOTEL & RESTAURANT
होटल एवं रेस्तराँ

1. Which is the best hotel in this city?	इस शहर का सबसे अच्छा होटल कौन सा है?	Is shahar kā sabse achchhā hotal kaun sā hai?
2. I need a single bed room with attached bath.	मुझे गुसलखाने के साथ लगा एक बिस्तर वाला कमरा चाहिए।	Mujhe gusalkhāne ke sāth lagā ek bistar wālā kamrā chāhiye.
3. Will this room suit you?	यह कमरा क्या आपको पसंद है?	Yah kamrā kyā apko pasaṅd hai?
4. How much does this room cost per day?	इस कमरे का एक दिन का किराया कितना है?	Is kamre kā ek din ka kirāyā kitnā hai?
5. I shall stay for two weeks.	मैं दो सप्ताह तक ठहरूंगा।	Maiṅ do saptāh tak ṭhahrūngā.
6. The charges for the room is thirty rupees per day.	इस कमरे का किराया तीस रुपये प्रतिदिन है।	Is kamre kā kirāyā tis rupaye pratidin hai.

7. Can I have a hot water bath?	क्या मैं गर्म पानी से नहा सकता हूं? hūṅ?	Kyā maiṅ garm pāni se nahā sakta
8. Send the room boy to me.	बैरे को मेरे कमरे में भेजिए। bhejiye.	Baire ko mere kamre meiṅ
9. Is there any letter for me?	क्या मेरे लिए कोई पत्र है?	Kyā mere liye koi patra hai?
10. I want another blanket.	मुझे दूसरा कम्बल चाहिए।	Mujhe dusrā kambal chāhiye.
11. Change the sheets.	चादर बदल दीजिए।	Chādar badal dijiye.
12. I want one more pillow.	मुझे एक तकिया और चाहिए।	Mujhe ek takiyā aur chāhiye.
13. Is there any phone for me?	क्या मेरे लिए कोई फोन है?	Kyā mere liye koi phon hai?
14. Please have the room swept.	कृपया कमरा साफ करवा दीजिए।	Kripayā kamrā sāf karwā dijiye.
15. Please bring some postage stamps from the post-office.	कृपया डाकखाने से कुछ डाक-टिकटें ला दीजिए।	Kripayā dāk khāna se kuchh dāk tikateṅ la dijiye.
16. Give some fruits for me.	मेरे लिए कुछ फल ले आना।	Mere liye kuchh phal le ānā.
17. Please give me lunch at 1P.M. and dinner at 9 P.M.	कृपया दोपहर का भोजन एक बजे और रात का भोजन नौ बजे दीजिए।	Kripayā dopahar kā bhojan ek baje aur rāt kā bhojan nau baje dijiye.

18. What are the charges for lunch and dinner?	दोपहर और रात के भोजन के कितने पैसे लगेंगे?	Dopahar aur rāt ke bhojan ke kitne paise lagenge?
19. We change seven rupees for each diet.	हम प्रत्येक खुराक के सात रुपये लेते हैं।	Ham pratyek khurāk ke sat rupaye lete haiṅ.
20. Have you a swimming pool?	क्या आपके यहां तैरने के लिए तालाब है?	Kyā apke yahāṅ tairne ke liya tālāb hai?
21. Is there an extra charge for swimming?	क्या तैरने का अलग से लेते हैं?	Kyā tairne kā alag se lete haiṅ?
22. Is the hotel open for twenty four hours?	क्या होटल चौबीस घंटे खुला रहता है।	Kyā hotal chaubis ghaṅte khulā rahtā hai?
23. I shall leave early tomorrow.	मैं कल सुबह जल्दी चला जाऊंगा।	Maiṅ kal subah jaldi chalā jāoṅgā.
24. Bring the bill.	बिल लाइए।	Bil lāiye.
25. There is a mistake in the bill.	इस बिल में गलती है।	Is bill meiṅ galti hai.
26. I never ordered the wine.	मैंने कभी शराब नहीं मंगाई।	Maine kabhi sharāb nahiṅ maṅgai.
27. You have included wine in the bill wrongly.	आपने बिल में गलती से शराब के पैसे लगा दिए हैं।	Āpne bil meṅ galti se sharāb ke paise lagā diye hain.
28. Call the porter.	सामान उठाने वाले को बुलाइए।	Sāmān uṭhāne wāle ko bulāiye.

29. Do you accept cheques?	क्या आप चेक लेते हैं?	Kyā āp chek lete haiṅ?
30. No, we accept only cash.	नहीं, हम केवल नकद लेते है।	Ham kewal nakad lete haiṅ.
31. Please get me a taxi.	कृपया मेरे लिए टैक्सी मंगाइए।	Kripayā mere liya taixi maṅgāiye.
32. Please ring to the airport to know the timing of Delhi flight.	कृपया एयरपोर्ट पर फोन करके दिल्ली की फ्लाइट का समय पूछिए।	Kripayā eyarport par phon karke Dilli ki flaiṭ kā samay pūchhiye.
33. I shall come again next month.	मैं अगले माह फिर आऊंगा।	Maiṅ agle māh phir āūṅgā.
34. Thanks for the best services provided by you.	बेहतरीन सुविधाओं के लिए आपका धन्यवाद।	Behtarin suvidhāoṅ ke liye āpkā dhanyavād.
35. You are welcome, sir.	आपका स्वागत है, श्रीमान।	Āpkā swāgat hai shrimān!

36TH STEP छत्तीसवीं सीढ़ी

POST OFFICE/ TELEPHONE/BANK
डाकघर/टेलीफोन/बैंक

Post Office डाकघर

1.	Where can I find a post-office?	डाकघर किधर है?	Dāk-ghar kidhar hai?
2.	Please weight this parcel.	कृपया इस पार्सल का भार तौलिए।	Kripayā is pārsal kā bhār toliye.
3.	I want to send some money by the mony order.	मैं मनीऑर्डर द्वारा कुछ पैसे भेजना चाहता हूं।	Maiṅ maniardar dwārā kuchh paise bhejnā chahtā huṅ.
4.	I want to deposit Rs. two hundred only.	मैं केवल दो सौ रुपये जमा कराना चाहता हूं।	Maiṅ kewal do sau rupaye jamā karānā chāhtā hūṅ.
5.	I want to draw out Rs. three hundred only.	मैं केवल तीन सौ रुपये निकलवाना चाहता हूं।	Maiṅ kewal tin sau rupaye nikalwānā chāhtā hūṅ.
6.	Please give me an Inland Letter.	कृपया मुझे एक अंतर्देशीय पत्र दीजिए।	Kripayā mujhe ek antardeshiy patra dijiye.

7. How much is for an envelope?	एक लिफाफे की क्या कीमत है?	Ek lifāfe ki kyā kimat hai?
8. I want to send it by the registered post.	मैं इसे रजिस्टर्ड डाक द्वारा भेजना चाहता हूं।	Maiṅ ise rajistard dāk dwārā bhejnā chāhtā hūṅ.
9. How much should I give for a post card?	मैं एक पोस्ट कार्ड के लिए कितने पैसे दूं?	maiṅ ek poṣt kard ke liya kitne paise dūṅ?
10. Please give me one rupee postal stamp.	कृपया मुझे एक रुपये की डाक-टिकट दीजिए।	Kripayā mujhe ek rupaye ke dāk-takat dijiye.
11. I want to send a telegram.	मैं एक टेलीग्राम देना चाहता हूं।	Maiṅ ek ṭeligram denā chāhtā hūṅ.
12. I want to send some money telegraphically.	मैं तार द्वारा पैसे भेजना चाहता हूं।	Maiṅ tār dwārā paise bhejnā chāhtā hūṅ.
13. Please give me an aerogram for France.	कृपया मुझे फ्रांस के लिए डाक-पत्र दीजिए।	Kripayā mujhe Frāns ke liye dāk-patra dijiye.
14. Please give me the telephone directory.	कृपया मुझे टेलीफोन डायरेक्टरी देना।	Kripayā mujhe Telephone dāyrektory denā.

Telephone टेलीफोन (दूरभाष)

15. Where can I ring up?	मैं टेलीफोन कहां से कर सकता हूं?	Maiṅ teliphon kahāṅ se kar saktā hūṅ?
16. This telephone is out of order.	यह टेलीफोन खराब है।	Yah teliphon kharāb hai

17. I want to book a trunk call for Bhubaneswar.	मैं एक ट्रंक काल भुवनेश्वर करना चाहती हूं।	Maiṅ ek trank kāl Bhubaneshwar karnā chāhti hūṅ.
18. Hellow, this is Abha here.	हेलो! मैं आभा बोल रही हूं।	Helo! Maiṅ Ābhā bol rahi hūṅ.
19. May I talk to Minakshi?	मीनाक्षी को बुला दीजिए।	Mainaksi ko bulā dijiye.
20. Hellow, Minakshi speaking.	हेलो, मीनाक्षी बोल रही हूं।	Helo, Minakshi bol. rahi hūṅ.
21. Please ring me at 8 o'clock.	कृपया आठ बजे फोन कीजिए।	Kripayā āth baje phon kijiye.

Bank बैंक

22. Where is the Indian Overseas Bank?	इंडियन ओवरसीज़ बैंक कहां है?	Indian Ovarsiz Bank kahān hai?
23. Can I meet the manager?	क्या मैं मैनेजर से मिल सकता हूं?	Kyā maiṅ mainejar se mil saktā hūṅ?
24. I want to open a saving bank account.	मैं एक बचत खाता खोलना चाहता हूं।	Main ek bachat-khātā kholnā chāhtā hūṅ.
25. Please open a current account in the name of my firm.	कृपया मेरी फर्म के नाम एक चालू खाता खोलिए।	Kripayā mere farm ke nām ek chālu khātā kholiye.
26. I want to deposit money.	मैं पैसे जमा कराना चाहता हूं।	Maiṅ paise jamā karānā chāhatā hūṅ.
27. I want to draw out money.	मैं पैसे निकालना चाहता हूं।	Maiṅ paise nikālanā chāhtā hun.

28. Please give me a loose cheque.	कृपया एक खुला चैक दीजिए।	Kripayā ek khulā chek dijiye.
29. Please issue me a cheque book containing ten cheques.	कृपया मुझे दस चैक वाली एक चैक बुक जारी कीजिए।	Kripayā mujhe das chek wali ek chek-buk jāri kijiye.
30. Please tell me the balance of my account.	कृपया मेरे खाते की जमा राशि बताइए।	Kripayā mere khāte ki jamā rāshi batāiye.
31. Please complete my pass book.	कृपया मेरी पास बुक पूरी करके दें।	Kripayā meri pās-buk pūri karke deṅ.
32. I want some loan for buying a colour television.	मुझे एक रंगीन टेलीविजन खरीदने के लिए ऋण चाहिए।	Mujhe ek raṅgin telivizan kharidne ke liye riṅ chāhiye.
33. I want to meet the agent.	मैं एजेंट से मिलना चाहता हूं।	Maiṅ ejent se milnā chāhtā hūṅ.
34. Is there any of my cheque dishonoured?	क्या मेरा कोई चैक वापिस आया है?	Kyā merā koi chek vāpis āyā hai?
35. Service of this bank is very good.	इस बैंक की सेवा बड़ी अच्छी है।	Is bānk ki sewā bari achchhi hai.

37TH STEP सैंतीसवीं सीढ़ी

WHILE TRAVELLING

यात्रा करते समय

1.	I am going out for a ride.	मैं घुड़सवारी करने जा रहा हूं।	Maiṅ ghuṛswāri karne jā rahā hūṅ.
2.	Where is the stable?	अस्तबल कहां है?	Astbal kahāṅ hai?
3.	I want to dismount for a while.	मुझे थोड़ी देर के लिए उतरना है।	Mujhe thoṛi der ke liye utarnā hai.
4.	Don't whip him.	उसे चाबुक मत मारो।	Use chābuk mat māro.
5.	Give him some grass.	उसे थोड़ी घास दो।	Use thoṛi ghās do.
6.	Take off the spurs.	कांटे निकालो।	Kaṅṭe nikālo.
7.	I wish to go by car.	मैं कार से जाना चाहता हूं।	Maiṅ kār se jānā chātā hūṅ.
8.	Its wheel is not good.	इसका पहिया अच्छा नहीं है।	Iskā pahiyā achchhā nahiṅ hai.
9.	Where does this road lead to?	यह रास्ता किधर को जाता है?	Yah rāstā kidhar ko jātā hai.

10. Leave the car here.	गाड़ी इधर रखो।	Gāri idhar rakho.
11. Parking is prohibited.	वाहन खड़ा करना मना है।	Vāhan khaṛa karnā manā hai.
12. Does this tramway pass near the railway station?	क्या इस ट्राम की पटरी रेलवे स्टेशन से होकर जाती है।	Kyā is trām ki patri relwe steshan se hokar jāti hai?
13. When will this bus start?	यह बस कब चलेगी?	Yah bas kab chalegi?
14. Let me know when we shall reach Kashmir.	मुझे बताइए, हम कश्मीर कब पहुंचेंगे?	Mujhe batāiye, ham Kāshmir kab pahuṅcheṅge.
15. I wish to roam by shikara.	मैं शिकारा में सैर करना चाहता हूं।	Maiṅ shikārā meiṅ sair karnā chāhtā hūṅ.
16. Where is the booking office?	टिकट मिलने की जगह कहां है?	Tikaṭ milne ki jagah kahāṅ hai?
17. Is there anything worth seeing?	क्या वहां कोई दर्शनीय स्थल है?	Kyā yahāṅ koi darshaniy sthal hai?
18. Kindly move a little.	कृपा करके थोड़ा हट जाइए।	Kripā karke thoṛā haṭ jāiye.
19. I am going to Bombay today.	आज मैं बम्बई जा रहा हूं।	Āj maiṅ Bambay jā rahā hūṅ.
20. When does the next train start?	अगली गाड़ी कितने बजे छूटती है।	Agali gāṛi kitne baje chūṭati hai.

21. Where is the luggage booking office?	सामान बुक करवाने का दफ्तर कहां है?	Sāmān buk karwāne kā daftar kahān hai?
22. How much to pay for luggage?	सामान के लिए कितने पैसे देने हैं?	Sāmān ke liye kitne paise dene haiṅ?
23. Get my seat reserved.	मेरा स्थान आरक्षित कर दीजिए।	Merā sthān ārakṣit kar dijiye.
24. Where is the platform No.6?	प्लेटफार्म नं. 6 कहाँ है?	Platfarm no. 6 kahāṅ hai?
25. Over the bridge.	पुल के उस पार।	Pul ke us pār.
26. Please go by the underground passage.	जमीन के नीचे के रास्ते से जाइए।	Zamin ke niche ke rāste se jāiye.
27. There is a dining car in the train.	गाड़ी में खाने का डिब्बा है।	Gāri meiṅ khāne ka dibbā hai.
28. There is no seat available	कोई सीट खाली नहीं है।	Koi sit khāli nahin hai.
29. The bus is very crowded.	बस में बहुत भीड़ है।	Bas meiṅ bahut bhiṛ hai.
30. Do not get down from the running bus.	चलती बस से मत उतरिए।	Chalti bus se mat utariye.
31. Our bus is in motion.	हमारी बस चल रही है।	Hamari bas chal rahi hai.
32. How much do you charge for a child?	बच्चे का कितना किराया लेते हैं?	Bachche kā kitnā kirāyā lete haiṅ?

33. Take me to the aerodrome.	मुझे हवाई अड्डे पर ले चलिए।	Mujhe hawāi adde par le chaliye.
34. Please issue me a return ticket for Singapore.	कृपया सिंगापुर जाने और वापिस आने का टिकट दीजिए।	Kripayā mujhe Singā pur jāne aur vāpis āne kā ṭikaṭ dijiye.
35. Our plane reached Singapore in time.	हमारा जहाज ठीक समय पर सिंगापुर पहुंच गया।	Hamārā jahāz thik samay par Singāpur pahuāch gayā.

38TH STEP अड़तीसवीं सीढ़ी

HEALTH & HYGIENE
स्वास्थ्य एवं स्वास्थ्य रक्षा

1.	Health is wealth.	स्वास्थ्य धन है।	Swāsthya dhan hai.
2.	Prevention is better than cure.	इलाज से परहेज बेहतर है।	Ilāj se parhez behtar hai.
3.	She is very tired.	वह बहुत थकी हुई है।	Vah bahut thaki hui hai.
4.	My health has broken down.	मेरा स्वास्थ्य गिर गया है।	Merā swāsthya gir gayā hai.
5.	He has recovered.	वह स्वस्थ हो गया है।	Vah swastha ho gayā hai.
6.	I am feeling sleepy.	मुझे नींद आ रही है।	Mujhe niṅd ā rahi hai.
7.	We should not sleep in day time	हमें दिन में नहीं सोना चाहिए।	Hameṅ din meiṅ nahiṅ sonā chāhiye.
8.	Will you come for a walk?	आप टहलने चलेंगे न?	Āp tahalne chaleṅge na?
9.	He is better than yesterday.	वह कल से आज अच्छा है।	Vah kal se āj achchhā hai.

10. I am not well today.	आज मेरी तबियत ठीक नहीं।	Āj meri tabiyat thik nahiṅ.
11. Will you not take the medicine?	क्या तुम दवा नहीं लोगी?	Kyā tum dawā nahiṅ logi.
12. How is your father?	आपके पिता जी कैसे हैं?	Āp ke pitāji kaise haiṅ.

Doctor & Patient डॉक्टर और रोगी

13. Let me feel your pulse.	मुझे अपनी नब्ज देखने दो।	Mujhe apni nabza dekhne do.
14. I am feeling out of sorts today.	मेरी तबियत खराब है।	Meri tabiyat kharab hai.
15. The patient is sinking.	बीमार का दिल कमजोर हो रहा है।	Bimār kā dil kamjor ho rahā hai.
16. I suffer from indigestion.	मेरा हाजमा बिगड़ा हुआ है।	Merā hāzmā bigṛā hua hai.
17. She feels nousea.	उसका जी मतला रहा है।	Uskā ji matlā raha hai.
18. Do you feel dizzy?	क्या तुम्हारा सिर चकरा रहा है?	Kyā tumhārā sir chakrā rahā hai?
19. She is out of danger now.	उसे अब कोई खतरा नहीं।	Use ab koi khatrā nahiṅ.
20. The child is cutting the teeth.	बच्चे का दांत निकल रहा है।	Bachche ka dānt nikal raha hai.
21. How many doses have you taken?	तुमने कितनी खुराकें ली हैं?	Tumne kitni khurākeṅ li haiṅ?

22. I suffer from severe constipation.	मुझे सख्त कब्ज की शिकायत है।	Mujhe sakht kabz ki shikāyat hai.
23. You had a chronic fever.	तुम्हें पुराना बुखार था।	Tumheṅ purānā bukhār thā.
24. I have sore-throat.	मुझे गले की शिकायत है।	Mujhe gale ki shikayat hai.
25. Had she a headache?	क्या उसे सिरदर्द था?	Kya use sirdard tha?
26. She has pain in her stomach.	उसके पेट में दर्द है।	Uske peṭ meiṅ dard hai.
27. Is he suffering from cold?	उसे जुकाम हुआ है क्या?	Use zukām huā hai kyā?
28. Show me your tongue?	मुझे अपनी जबान दिखाओ।	Mujhe apni zabān dikhāo.
29. She has lost her appetite.	उसकी भूख मारी गई है।	Uski bhūkh mari gayi hai.
30. I have got a boil.	मुझे फोड़ा हुआ है।	Mujhe phoṛā huā hai.
31. Her gums are bleeding.	उसके मसूड़ों से खून निकलता है।	Uske masūṛon se khūn nikaltā hai.
32. Send for a doctor.	डॉक्टर को बुलाओ।	Daktar ko bulāo.
33. She has pain in the liver.	उसके कलेजे में पीड़ा है।	Uske kaleje meṅ pirā hai.
34. You shall have some motions.	तुम्हें कुछ दस्त होंगे।	Tumheṅ kuchh dast hoṅge.
35. The physician will call next morning.	चिकित्सक अगली सुबह आएँगे।	Chikitsak agli subah ayeṅge.

39TH STEP उनतालीसवीं सीढ़ी

WEATHER
मौसम

1. It is spring season.	वसंत ऋतु है।	Vasant ritu hai.
2. It is summer.	ग्रीष्म ऋतु है।	Grism ritu hai.
3. It is autumn.	पतझड़ ऋतु है।	Patjhaṛ ritu hai.
4. It is winter.	शीत ऋतु है।	Shit ritu hai.
5. It very hot today.	आज बड़ी गर्मी है।	Āj baṛi garmi hai.
6. It is very cold day.	बहुत ठण्डा दिन है।	Bahut ṭhan̐da din hai.
7. This is fine weather.	सुहावना दिन है।	Suhāvnā din hai.
8. What wretched day!	आज कितना खराब दिन है।	Āj kitnā kharāb din hai.
9. It is raining.	वर्षा हो रही है।	Varṣā ho rahi hai.
10. It is drizzing.	बूंदाबांदी हो रही है।	Bundābāndi ho rahi hai.
11. Has the moon risen?	चांद निकला है क्या?	Chān̐d niklā hai kyā?

12. It has stopped raining.	वर्षा बंद हो गई है।	Varṣā baṅd ho gayi hai.
13. She will catch cold.	उसे सर्दी लग जायेगी।	Use sardi lag jayegi.
14. Does it still rain?	अब तक पानी बरस रहा है क्या?	Ab tak pāni bars rahā hai kyā?
15. In rainy season, we wear raincoat.	बरसात के मौसम में हम बरसाती पहनते हैं।	Barsāt ke mausam meiṅ ham barasāti pahante haiṅ.
16. I am shivering.	मैं कांप रहा हूं।	Maiṅ kāṅp rahā hūṅ.
17. I am perspiring.	मुझे पसीना आ रहा है।	Mujhe pasinā ā rahā hai.
18. I am drenched.	मैं भीग गया हूं।	Maiṅ bhig gayā hūṅ.
19. Cool air is blowing.	शीतल वायु बह रही है।	Shital vāyu bah rahi hai.
20. What a strong wind!	कितनी तेज हवा है!	Kitni tez hava hai!
21. The weather is changing.	मौसम बदल रहा है।	Mausam badal rahā hai.
22. The sky is cloudy.	आकाश बादलों से ढका है।	Ākāsh bādloṅ se dhakā hai.
23. The sky is cloudy.	आसमान साफ है।	Asmān sāf hai.
24. It lightens.	बिजली चमकती है।	Bijli chamakti hai.
25. It thunders.	बादल गरजते हैं।	Bādal garajte hain.
26. The sun is invisible.	सूरज दिखाई नहीं देता है।	Suraj dikhāyī nahiṅ detā hai.

27. It is like a spring day.	बसंत का सा दिन है।	Basant ka sā din hai.
28. The heat is unbearable.	गर्मी असहनीय है।	Garmi asahniy hai.
29. It is bright fortnight.	यह शुक्ल पक्ष है।	Yah shukla pakṣa hai.
30. It is later part of the night.	आधी रात के बाद का समय है।	Ādhi rāt ke bād kā samay hai.
31. What a beautiful the rainbow is!	इन्द्रधनुष कितना सुंदर है!	Indradhanus kitnā sunder hai!
32. It is raining in heavy torrents.	मूसलाधार वर्षा हो रही है।	Mūslādhār varsā ho rahe hai.
33. It is hailing badly.	बुरी तरह से ओले पड़ रहे हैं।	Buri tarah se ole paṛ rahe haiṅ.
34. Would you like an umbrella?	क्या आप छाता लेंगे।	Kyā āp chhātā leṅge.
35. What a fine the climate is!	जलवायु कितना मोहक है!	Jalvāyu kitṅā mohak hai!

40TH STEP चालीसवीं सीढ़ी

TIME
समय

1. Look at the watch.	घड़ी देखो।	Ghaṛi dekho.
2. What is the time?	क्या बजा है?	Kyā bajā hai?
3. What is the time by your watch?	आपकी घड़ी में क्या बजा है?	Āpki ghaṛi meiṅ kyā baja hai?
4. What o'clock is it?	कितने बजे हैं?	Kitne baje haiṅ?
5. It is exactly 7 o'clock.	ठीक सात बजे हैं।	Ṭhik sāt baje haiṅ.
6. It is half past nine.	साढ़े नौ बजे हैं।	Saṛhe nau baje haiṅ.
7. It is quarter past three.	सवा तीन बजे हैं।	Savā tin baje haiṅ.
8. It is quarter to four.	पौने चार बजे हैं।	Paune chār baje haiṅ.
9. It is five minutes past five.	पांच बजकर पांच मिनट हुए हैं।	Pāṅch bajkar pāṅch minat hue haiṅ.
10. It is ten minutes to six.	छह बजने में दस मिनट है।	Chhah bajne mein das minut hue haiṅ.

11. It is already half past four.	साढ़े चार बजे चुके हैं।	Saṛhe chār baj chuke haiṅ.
12. She will reach at one and a quarter o'clock.	वह सवा एक बजे पहुंचेगी।	Vah savā ek baje pahūṅchegi.
13. We reached the office at twenty-five minutes past ten.	हम दस बजकर पचीस मिनट पर कार्यालय पहुंचे।	Ham das bajkar pachiṣ minaṭ par karyālay pahuṅche.
14. The bank was looted in the broad daylight.	बैंक दिन-दहाड़े लूट लिया गया।	Baiṅk din-dahāṛe lūt liyā gayā.
15. The market is closed Monday.	बाजार सोमवार को बंद रहता है।	Bāzār somvar ko baṅd rahta hai.
16. We take lunch at half past one.	हम डेढ़ बजे दोपहर का भोजन करते हैं।	Ham ḍeḍh baje dophar kā bhojan karte haiṅ.
17. This shop reopens at half past two.	यह दुकान ढाई बजे दुबारा खुलती है।	Yah dukān ḍhai baje dubārā khulti hai.
18. It is ten A.M.	सवेरे के दस बजे हैं।	Swere ke das baje haiṅ.
19. We leave the office exactly at five P.M.	हमें दफ्तर से ठीक पांच बजे छुट्टी मिलती है।	Hameṅ dafter se ṭhik pāṅch baje chūṭṭi milti hai.
20. Is your wrist watch slow?	क्या तुम्हारी कलाई-घड़ी सुस्त है?	Kyā tumhāri kalāi-ghaṛi sust hai?
21. Is this time-piece fast?	क्या यह मेज-घड़ी तेज है?	Kyā yah mez-ghaṛi tez hai?
22. Is the office-clock not exact?	क्या कार्यालय की दीवार घड़ी ठीक नहीं है?	Kyā kāryālay ki diwar-ghaṛi ṭhik nahiṅ hai?

23. My pen watch has stopped.	मेरी पेन-घड़ी बंद हो गई है।	Meri pen-ghaṛi baṅd ho gayi, hai.
24. It is time to rise.	जागने का समय हो गया।	Jagne kā samay ho gayā.
25. You are half an hour late.	आपको आधा घंटा देर हो गई।	Āpko ādhā ghaṇtā der ho gayi.
26. She is ten minutes early.	वह दस मिनट जल्दी आई है।	Veh das minaṭ jaldi āyi hai.
27. It is midnight.	आधी रात का समय है।	Ādhi rāt ka samay hai.
28. My mother gets up early in the morning.	मेरी माताजी प्रातः बहुत जल्दी उठती हैं।	Meri mātāji prātaḥ bahut jaldi uṭhati haiṅ.
29. Last month, we were not here.	पिछले महीने हम यहां नहीं थे।	Pichhle mahine ham yahāṅ nahiṅ the.
30. We shall remain here this month.	इस महीने हम यहां रहेंगे।	Is mahine ham yahāṅ raheṅge.
31. I shall go to Simla next month.	मैं अगले महीने शिमला जाऊंगा।	Maiṅ agle mahine Shimlā jaūṅgā.
32. We are in trouble since 15th August.	हम 15 अगस्त से संकट में हैं।	Ham 15 Agast se saṅkaṭ meṅ haiṅ.
33. What is the date today?	आज क्या तारीख है?	Āj kyā tārikh-hai?
34. Why had you come yesterday?	कल तुम क्यों आए थे?	Kal tum kyoṅ āye the?
35. Come tomorrow at 7 o'clock.	कल सात बजे आना।	Kal sāt baje ānā.

PART 5
CONVERSATION

41ST STEP इकतालीसवां सीढ़ी

LET US TALK
आओ, बातचीत करें

INTRODUCTION परिचय

How do you do	आपका क्या हाल-चाल है?	Āpkā kyā hal-chal hai?
Tell me, please, are you a student?	कहिए, (क्या) आप छात्र हैं?	Kahiye, (kyā) āp chhātra haiṅ?
Yes, I am a student.	जी हाँ, मैं छात्र हूँ।	Ji hāṅ, maiṅ chhātra hūṅ.
What is your name?	आपका क्या नाम है?	Āpkā kyā nām hai?
My name is Pranav Chakaravarti.	मेरा नाम प्रणव चक्रवर्ती है।	Merā nām Praṇav Chahravarti hai.
Are you a Assame or a Bengali?	आप असमी है या बंगाली?	Āp asami haiṅ yā baṅgāli?
No, I am a Marathi.	नहीं, मैं मराठी हूं।	Nahiṅ, maiṅ marāṭhi hūṅ.
Tell me, please, who is she?	बताइए, वह कौन है?	Batāiye, vah kaun hai.
She is my friend Abha.	वह मेरी मित्र आभा है।	Vah meri mitra Ābhā hai.

Is she a student?	(क्या) वह छात्रा है?	(Kyā) vah chhātra hai.
No, she is a translator and works in the Govt. office.	नहीं, वह अनुवादक है और सरकारी कार्यालय में काम करती है।	Nahiṅ, vah anuvādak hai aur sarkāri kāryalay meiṅ kām karti hai.
Thanks, Good-bye.	धन्यवाद, विदा!	Dhanyavād, vida!

ABOUT LEARING LANGUAGE भाषा सीखने के बारे में

Hello, do you speak Hindi?	महोदय, (क्या) आप हिंदी बोलते हैं?	Mahoday, (kyā) āp Hindi bolte haiṅ?
Yes, I speak Hindi a little.	हां, मैं थोड़ी-थोड़ी हिंदी बोलता हूं।	Haṅ, maiṅ thôṛi-thôṛi Hindi boltā hūṅ.
You speak Hindi well	आप हिंदी बड़ी अच्छी बोलते हैं।	Āp Hindi baṛi achchhi bolte hain.
What is your caste?	आपकी जाति क्या है?	Āpki jāti kyā hai?
My caste is Kelkar. I am Ashok Kelkar.	मेरी जाति केलकर है। मैं अशोक केलकर हूं।	Meri jāti kelkar hai. Maiṅ Ashôk Kelkar hūṅ.
Do you think so? I am studying Hindi in college. I want to speak Hindi well.	आप ऐसा सोचते है? कालेज में हिंदी पढ़ रहा हूं। मैं हिंदी अच्छी तरह बोलना चाहता हूं।	Āp aisā sochte haiṅ? Maiṅ kālej meiṅ Hindi paṛh rahā hūṅ. Maiṅ Hindi achchhi tarah bôlnā chāhtā hūṅ?
Does your Hindi teacher speak Hindi in class?	क्या आपके हिंदी शिक्षक कक्षा में बोलते हैं?	Kyā āpke Hindi shikṣak kakṣā meiṅ bôlte haiṅ?
Of course! He	निःसंदेह! वह	Ni:saṅdeh! vah

speaks Hindi fluently.	धाराप्रवाह हिंदी में बोलते हैं।	dhārā-pravāh Hindi meṅ bôlte haiṅ?
Do you understand when the teacher speaks Hindi?	जब शिक्षक हिंदी में बोलते हैं तो क्या आप उसे समझते हैं?	Jab shikṣak Hindi meiṅ bôlte haiṅ to kyā āp use samajhate haiṅ?
Yes, we understand when he speaks fast.	जी हां, जब वह तेज बोलते हैं तो हम समझ लेते हैं।	Ji hāṅ, job vah tej bôlte haiṅ to ham samajh lete haiṅ.
Do you speak Hindi at home?	(क्या) आप घर पर हिंदी में बोलते हैं?	(Kyā) Āp ghar par Hindi meiṅ bôlte haiṅ?
Of course not! My family members do not speak Hindi. They speak only Marathi. Therefore, we speak only Marathi at home.	बेशक नहीं! मेरे परिवार के सदस्य हिंदी में नहीं बोलते। वे केवल मराठी में बोलते हैं। इसलिए हम लोग घर में केवल मराठी में बोलते हैं।	Beshak nahiṅ! Mere parivār ke sadasya Hindi meiṅ nahiṅ bôlte. Ve kewel Marāṭhi meṅ bôlte haiṅ. Isliya ham log ghar meiṅ kewel Marāṭhi meṅ bôlte haiṅ.
But you speak Hindi very well!	परंतु आप हिंदी बहुत अच्छी बोलते हैं।	Paraṅtu āp Hindi bahut achchhi bôlte haiṅ.
Thank you very much!	आपका बहुत-बहुत धन्यवाद!	Āpakā bahut-bahut dhanyawād!

VILLAGE VERSUS CITY गाँव बनाम शहर

You live in the village, but go to	आप गाँव में रहते हैं, पर शहर में काम	Āp gāoṅ meṅ rahte haiṅ, par shahar

the city to work.	करने जाते हैं। (क्या)	meṅ kām karne jāte haiṅ. (Kyā) Āp
Do you prefer to live in the village?	आप गांव में रहना अधिक पसंद करते हैं?	gāoṅ meṅ rahnā adhik pasaṅd karte haiṅ?
Oh, yes! I prefer to live there. But I also like the city.	जी हां! मैं वहां रहना अधिक पसंद करता हू। पर मैं शहर को भी चाहता हूं।	Ji haṅ! Maiṅ vahaṅ rahnā adhik pasaṅd kartā hūṅ. Par maiṅ shahar ko bhi chāhta hūṅ.
Why do you like the city?	आप शहर को क्यों चाहते हैं?	Āp shahar ko kyoṅ chāhte haiṅ?
In the city, there are threatres, museums, libraries	शहर में सिनेमा-नाटक है, संग्रहालय, पुस्तकालय और	Shahar meiṅ, sinemā-natāk haiṅ, saṅgrahālay.
and university, etc.	विश्वविद्यालय आदि सभी कुछ हैं।	pustakālay aur Vishwavidyālay adi sabhi kuchh haiṅ.
But there are also factories, buses, trucks and cars. Everywhere there are crowds and noise.	परन्तु वहां कारखाने बसें, ट्रक, कारें भी हैं। हर जगह शोर-गुल होता है।	Parantu vahāṅ kārkhane baseṅ, trak, kareṅ bhi haiṅ. Har jagah shor-gul hotā hai.
Quite right. That is why I prefer to live in the village, although I do work in the city. In the village, it is quiiet, the air is fresh.	यह ठीक है। यही कारण है कि मैं गांव में रहना अधिक अच्छा समझता हूं, यद्यपि मैं शहर में काम करता हूं। गांव में शांति होती	Yah ṭhik hai. Yahi kāran hai ki maiṅ gāoṅ meiṅ rahnā adhik achchhā samajhatā hūṅ, yadyapi maiṅ shahr meiṅ kām karta hūṅ

	है। हवा स्वच्छ होती है।	Gāoṅ meṅ shānti hoti hai. Hawā swachchh hoti hai.
And does your wife like life in the vallage?	और (क्या) आपकी पत्नी भी गांव की जिंदगी पसंद करती हैं?	Aur (kyā) āpkī patni bhi gāoṅ ki zindgi pasaṅd karti haiṅ?
She likes it very much. However, now and then she goes to the city to buy clothes and other things.	वह इसे बहुत पसंद करती है। वैसे जब-तब वह कपड़े तथा दूसरी चीजें खरीदने शहर जाती है।	Vah ise pasaṅd karti hai. Vaise jab-tāb vah kapare tathā dūṣri chizeṅ kharidne shahar jāti haiṅ.
However, our family members are happy in the village.	इस पर भी, हमारे परिवार के सदस्य गांव में प्रसन्न हैं।	Is par bhi, hamāre parivār ke sadasya gāoṅ meiṅ prasanna haiṅ.

LEARNING OF LANGUAGE भाषा सीखना

Hello, Nambiar, how are you?	श्री नंबियार महोदय आप कैसे हैं?	Shri Nambiār mahoday ap kaise haiṅ?
Very well, thank you.	बिलकुल ठीक-ठाक हूं। धन्यवाद।	Bikul ṭhik-ṭhāk hūṅ. Dhanyavād!
And how is your family?	और आपका परिवार कैसा है?	Aur āpkā pariwār kaisā hai?
Thanks, all are well.	आपकी मेहरबानी से सब ठीक-ठाक है।	Āpki meharbāni se sab ṭhik-ṭhak haiṅ.
By the way, I hear that you have been	वैसे, मैंने सुना है कि कुछ समय से आप	Vaise maiñne sunā hai ki kuchh samay

studying Hindi for sometime now.	हिंदी सीख रहे हैं।	se āp Hindi sikh rahe haiṅ.
That is true, I want to read, speak and write Hindi.	यह सच है, मैं हिंदी पढ़ना, बोलना और लिखना चाहता हूं।	Yah sach hai, maiṅ Hindi paṛhnā, bolnā aur likhnā chāhtā hūṅ.
Do you find that Hindi language is difficult?	(क्या) आपको लगता है कि हिंदी भाषा कठिन है?	(Kyā) Āpko lagtā hai ki Hindi bhāṣa kaṭhin hai?
It seems difficult to foreigners; but I am making progress.	विदेशियों को वह कठिन लगती है, पर मैं प्रगति कर रहा हूं।	Videshioṅ ko vah kaṭhin lagti hai; par maiṅ pragati kar rahā hūṅ.
Excellent! you are already speaking Hindi well.	बहुत अच्छे! आप तो पहले ही हिंदी अच्छी बोलते हैं।	Bahut achchhe! Āp to pahle hi Hindi achchhi bolte haiṅ.
Thanks! I want to speak still better.	धन्यवाद! मैं और भी अच्छा बोलना चाहता हूं।	Dhanyavād! Maiṅ aur bhi achchhā bolnā chāhtā hūṅ.
Your enthusiasm is praiseworthy.	आपका उत्साह प्रशंसा योग्य है।	Āpkā utsāh prasha-ṅsā yogya hai.

42ND STEP बयालीसवीं सीढ़ी

BETWEEN TWO FRIENDS
दो मित्रों के बीच

Minakshi—Hello. How are you madam?	मीनाश्री-आप कैसी है श्रीमती?	— Āp kaisi haiṅ Shrimati?
Garima—Pretty well, thanks. And you?	गरिमा-ठीक-ठाक हूं आपकी कृपा है। और आप?	— Ṭhik-ṭhak hūṅ āpki kirpā hai. Aur āp?
Minakshi—I am fine, thanks.	मीनाक्षी-मैं ठीक से हूं। धन्यवाद!	— Main ṭhik se hūṅ, dhanyavād!
Garima—It's good to see you again.	गरिमा-अच्छा, फिर मिलेंगे।	— Achchha, phir mileṅge.

● ● ●

Abha—Do you watch television very often?	आभा-क्या तुम प्रायः दूरदर्शन देखते हो?	— Kyā tum prāyaḥ durdarshan dekhte ho?
Amit—Well, I some times watch it in the evening.	अमित-हां, मैं कभी-कभी इसे शाम को देखता हूं।	— Hāṅ, maiṅ kabhi-kabhi ise shām ko dekhta hūṅ.

Abha—Did you watch television last night?	आभा-क्या तुमने पिछली रात दूरदर्शन देखा था?	— Kyā tum ne pichhli rāt durdarshan dekhā thā?
Amit—Yes, I did, I saw several good programmes.	अमित-हां, देखा था। मैंने कुछ अच्छे कार्यक्रम देखे।	— Hāṅ, dekhā thā. Maiṅ ne kuchh achchhe kārya-kram dekhe.

● ● ●

Amit—Do you ever listen to the radio?	अमित-क्या तुम कभी आकाशवाणी सुनती हो?	— Kyā tum kabhi ākāshvāni sunti ho?
Abha—Certainly, I listen practically every night.	आभा-हां, अवश्य। मैं हर रात असल में आकाशवाणी सुनती हूं।	— Hāṅ, avashya. Maiṅ har rāt asal meṅ ākāshvāni sunti hūṅ.
Amit—What's your favourite programme?	अमित-तुम्हारा मनपसंद कार्यक्रम कौन-सा है?	— Tumhārā manpasaṅd kāryakram kaunsā hai?
Abha—I like vandanvar best of all.	आभा-मुझे वन्दनवार सबसे अच्छा लगता है।	— Mujhe vandanvār sabse achchhā lagtā hai.

● ● ●

Shehnaz—Where did you go?	शहनाज-तुम कहां गई थीं?	— Tum kahāṅ gayiṅ thiṅ?
Minaz—We went to a beautiful beach.	मीनाज-हम सुंदर समुद्र तट पर गई थीं।	— Ham sundar samudra taṭ par gayi thiṅ.

Shahnaz—Did you swim in the ocean?	शहनाज-क्या तुम समुद्र में तैरी थीं?	— Kyā tum samudra meiṅ ṭairi thiṅ?
Minaz—Yes, but I swam close to the shore!	मीनाज-हां, पर मैं किनारे के पास-पास तैरी थी।	— Hāṅ, par maiṅ kināre ke pās-pās ṭairi thi.
●	●	●
Manjula—What are you going to do tonight?	मंजुला-आज रात का, आप का क्या कार्यक्रम हैं?	— Āj rāt kā, āpkā kyā kārẏakram hai?
Gaurav—I have not decided yet.	गौरव-अभी मैंने निश्चय नहीं किया?	— Abhi maiṅne nishchay nahiṅ kiyā.
Manjula—Would you like to go the movies?	मंजुला-क्या आप सिनेमा जाना चाहेंगे?	— Kya ap sinemā janā chāheṅge?
Gaurav—No, I like to go to drama.	गौरव-नहीं, मैं नाटक देखना चाहूंगा।	— Nahiṅ, maiṅ naṭak dekhnā chāhūnga.
●	●	●
Manoj—I have to go to the railway station.	मनोज-मुझे रेलवे स्टेशन जाना है।	— Mujhe relwe steshan jānā hai.
Vikas—What do you have to go for?	विकास-तुम्हें वहां किसलिए जाना है?	— Tumheṅ vahāṅ kis liya jānā hai?
Manoj—To receive my sister from Bombay.	मनोज-मेरी बहन बंबई से आ रही है, उसे लेने जाना है।	— Meri bahan Bambai se ā rahi hai, use lene jānā hai.

Vikas—Let me take you in my scooter.	विकास-आओ मेरे स्कूटर पर बैठ चलो।	—	Āo mere skūṭar par baith chalo.
●	●		●
Pradip—Are you Dr. Bhartendu?	प्रदीप-क्या आप डॉ. भारतेंदु हैं?	—	Kyā āp Doctor Bhāratendu haiṅ?
Manohar—No. That tall fellow is Dr. Bharatendu	मनोहर-नहीं, वह लंबे महाशय डॉ. भारतेंदु हैं।	—	Nahiṅ? Vah lambe mahāshay Dr. Bhartendu. haiṅ?
Pradip—Do you mean the one over there with glasses?	प्रदीप-(क्या) आपका मतलब है, वह जो ऐनक पहने हैं?	—	(Kyā) Āpkā matlab hai, vah jo ainak pahne haiṅ?
Manohar—Yes. The one with dark hair.	मनोहर-हां, वह जो काले बालों वाले हैं।	—	Haṅ, vah jo kāle bāloṅ wale haiṅ.
●	●		●
Inamdar—How long have you been here?	ईनामदार-आप यहां कब से हैं?	—	Āp yahāṅ kab se haiṅ?
Gopal—I have been here for two weeks.	गोपाल-मैं दो सप्ताह से यहां हूं।	—	Maiṅ do saptah se yahāṅ hūṅ.
Inamdar—How often do you get here?	ईनामदार-आप कब-कब यहां आते हैं?	—	Ap kab-kab yahāṅ āte haiṅ?
Gopal—I get to this city about twice an year.	गोपाल-मैं लगभग वर्ष में दो बार इस शहर में आता हूं।	—	Maiṅ lagbhag varṣa meṅ do bār is shahr meṅ ātā hūṅ.

Anu—Did you have a good vacation?	अनु-क्या तुम्हारी छुट्टियाँ अच्छी बीतीं?	—	Kyā tumhāri chhuttiyāṅ achhchi bitiṅ?
Satya—Yes, I did. I had a wonderful time.	सत्य-हां, अच्छी बीतीं। वह समय बड़ा मजे का रहा।	—	Hāṅ, achchhi bitiṅ. Vah samay barā maze kā rahā.
Anu—What did you do?	अनु-तुम ने क्या किया?	—	Tumne kyā kiyā?
Satya—I visited some old friends in New Delhi.	सत्य-मैंने नई दिल्ली के कुछ पुराने मित्रों से भेंट की।	—	Maine Naī Dilli ke kuchh purane mitroṅ se bhent ki.

•••

43RD STEP तैंतालीसवां सीढ़ी

ABOUT MONEY
पैसे के बारे में

1.	How much money do you have?	तुम्हारे पास कितने रुपये हैं?	Tumhāre pās kitne rupaye haiṅ?
—	Not very much.	–बहुत अधिक नहीं।	— Bahut adhik nahiṅ?
	×	×	×
2.	She looks upset about something.	वह किसी बात पर परेशान दीखती हैं?	Vah kisī bāt par pareshān dikhti haiṅ?
—	I think she has lost her money? something.	–मुझे लगता है, उसके पैसे खो गए हैं।	–Mujhe lagtā hai uske paise kho gaye haiṅ?
—	Are you sure she lost her money?	–क्या आपको पक्का मालूम है कि उसके पैसे खो गए हैं?	— Kyā āpko pakkā malūm hai ki uske paise kho gaye haiṅ?
—	I am sure, she did.	–हां, मुझे विश्वास हैं।	— Hāṅ, mujhe vishwās hai.
	×	×	×

3.	How many rupees did you have in your bank?	अपने बैंक खाते में आपके कितने रुपये थे?	Āpne Baink khāte meṅ āpke kitne rupaye the?
—	I had exactly three hundred rupees.	–मेरे पास ठीक तीन सौ रुपये थे।	— Mere pās ṭhik tin sau rupaye the.
	×	×	×
4.	Did you sell your motorcycle?	क्या तुमने अपनी मोटरसाइकिल बेच दी?	Kyā tum ne apni motarsāikil bech di?
—	Yes, I sold it to my friend Anupam.	–हां, मैंने अपने मित्र अनुपम को बेच दी।	— Hāṅ; maiṅ ne apney mitra Anupam ko bech di.
	×	×	×
5.	Could you lend me one hundred rupees until tomorrow?	क्या आप कल तक के लिए एक सौ रुपये उधार दे सकेंगे?	Kyā āp kal tak ke liye ek sau rupaye udhār de sakeṅge?
—	Not, I could not.	–नहीं, मैं नहीं दे सकता।	— Nahiṅ, maiṅ nahiṅ de saktā.
	×	×	×
6.	Could you spare six hundred rupees?	क्या आप (मेरे लिए) छह सौ रुपये निकाल सकेंगे?	Kyā āp (mere liye) chhah sau rupaye nikāl sakeṅge?
—	Yes, but I shall need the money before next week.	–हां, पर मुझे वह पैसा अगले सप्ताह के पहले चाहिए।	— Hāṅ, par mujhe vah paisa agle saptāh ke pahle chāhiye.

7. Did you get the money?	क्या तुम्हें पैसा मिल गया?	Kyā tumheṅ paise mil gayā?
— Yes, I borrowed it form my colleague.	-हां, मैंने अपने साथी से उधार ले लिया।	— Hāṅ, maiṅne apne sāthi se udhār le liyā.
×	×	×
8. Have you got any change?	(क्या) आपके पास रेजगारी है?	(Kyā) āpke pās rezgāri hai?
— Here are seven coins of ten paise and six coins of five paise.	-मेरे पास सात सिक्के दस पैसे वाले और छः सिक्के पांच पैसे वाले हैं।	— Mere pās sāt sikke das paise wāle aur chhah sikke pāṅch paise wāle haiṅ.
×	×	×
9. Can you change this ten rupee note?	(क्या) आप यह दस रुपये वाला नोट बदल सकते हैं?	(Kyā) Āp yah das rupaye wālā not badal sakte haiṅ?
— I am sorry I don't have any note.	-खेद है, मेरे पास कोई नोट नहीं है।	— Khed hai, mere pās koi noṭ nahiṅ hai?
×	×	×
10. Do you have chang for one hundred rupees.	(क्या) आपके पास एक सौ रुपये के छोटे नोट हैं?	(Kyā) āpke pās ek sau rupaye ke chhote not haiṅ?
— Just a minute, and I shall see.	एक मिनट रुको, जरा देख लूं।	— Ek minat rūko, zarā dekh lūṅ.

11. Will you get foreign exchange?	(क्या) तुम विदेशी मुद्रा विनिमय करोगे?	(Kyā) tum videshi mudrā vinimay karoge?
— Yes, I will.	–हां, अवश्य।	— Hāṅ, avashya.
×	×	×
12. How much will you get?	आप कितनी राशि विनिमय करोगे?	Āp kitni rāshi vinimay karoge?
— A student generally gets foreign exchange worth about 5000 dollers per year.	–एक छात्र को प्रायः पांच हजार डालर प्रतिवर्ष विदेशी मुद्रा विनिमय प्राप्त होती है।	— Ek chhātra ko prah pāṅch hazār dollar prativarṣa videshi mudrā vinimay prāpt hoti hai.
×	×	×
13. What is your salary?	तुम्हारा वेतन कितना है?	Tumhārā vetan kitnā hai?
— I am drawing a salary of Rs. 400 per month.	–मुझे चार सौ रुपये प्रतिमाह वेतन मिलता है।	— Mujhe chār sau ruapaye pratimās vetan miltā hai?
×	×	×
14. How much do you expect?	आप कितनी राशि चाहते हैं?	Āp kitni rāṣi chāhte haiṅ?
— I do not wish to have more than fifty rupees.	–मैं पचास रुपये से अधिक नहीं पाना चाहता।	— Maiṅ pachās rupay se adhik nahiṅ pānā chāhta.
×	×	×
15. Do you give	आप कुछ कमीशन	Āp kuchh

any discount?	देंगे?	kamishan denge?
— Not at all.	-कुछ भी नहीं।	— Kuchh bi nahiṅ?
×	×	×
16. Is this worth twenty rupees?	क्या यह वस्तु बीस रुपये की होगी?	Kyā vah vastu bis rupaye ki hogi?
— Why not? It is rather costlier.	-क्यों नहीं? बल्कि यह तो और भी महंगी है।	— Kyoṅ nahiṅ? Balki yah to aur bhi mahṅgi hai.

44TH STEP चौवालीसवां सीढ़ी

ON THE BUS
बस में

1.	Pay for the tickets.	टिकटें ले लो।	Tikaṭṭeṅ le lo.
2.	No, I paid last time. It is your turn today.	नहीं, पिछली बार मैंने टिकटें ली थीं। आज तुम्हारी बारी है।	Nahiṅ, pichhli bar maiṅ ne tikaṭen li thiṅ. Āj tumhāri bāri hai.
3.	All right. Shall we get off at the ring road, Lajpat Nagar?	अच्छा। क्या हम रिंग रोड, लाजपतनगर उतरें?	Achchhā. Kyā ham Riṅg Road, Lājpat-nagar utreṅ?
4.	I think the Central Market is little nearer the Cinema. Anyway the fare is the same.	मैं तो समझता हूं, सेंट्रल मार्केट सिनेमा से थोड़ा पास पड़ता है। कुछ भी हो, किराया तो एक-सा है।	Maiṅ to samajhtā hūṅ, senṭral mārket sinema ke thoṛe pās paṛtā hai. Kuchh bhi ho kirāyā to ek-sā hai.
5.	Yes, it is. I usually get off at the Ring Road. But it makes no difference.	हां, ठीक है। मैं प्राय: रिंग रोड पर उतरता हूं। पर इससे कोई अंतर नहीं पड़ता।	Hāṅ, ṭhik hai. Maiṅ prāyah Riṅg Road par utartā hūṅ. Per isse koi antar nahiṅ paṛtā.

6.	Now buy tickets.	अब टिकटें ले लो।	Ab ṭikṭeṅ le lo.
7.	The bus is over crowded, So I think the conductor is very busy.	बस में भारी भीड़ है। सो मेरा विचार है, संवाहक बहुत व्यस्त हैं।	Bas men bhāri bhiṛ hai. So merā vichār hai samvāhak bahut vyasta hai.
8.	But have you got the money ready?	पर क्या तुमने पैसे निकाल लिए हैं?	Par kyā tumne paise nikāl liya haiṅ?
9.	Yes, I have got the exact fare.	हां, मेरे पास किराये के लिए खुले पैसे हैं।	Hāṅ, mere pās kiraye ke liye khule paise haiṅ.

IN A PUBLIC LIBRARY सार्वजनिक पुस्तकालय में

1.	May I be a regular member of the library?	क्या मैं पुस्तकालय का नियमित सदस्य बन सकता हूं?	Kyā maiṅ pustakālaya kā niyamit sadasya ban saktā hūṅ?
2.	Of course. Complete this form, please, and get it signed by any Gazetted officer.	निःसंदेह। यह फार्म भरिए और किसी राजपत्रित अधिकारी से हस्ताक्षर करवाइए।	Ni:saṅdeh. Yeh farm bhariye aur kisi rajpatrit adhikāri se hastākṣar karvāiye.
3.	What is the membership fees?	सदस्यता शुल्क कितना है?	Sadasyatā shulka kitnā hai?
4.	Not at all, the public library service is entirely free.	कुछ भी नहीं। सार्वजनिक पुस्तकालय सेवा सर्वथा निःशुल्क है।	Kuchh bhi nahiṅ Sarvjanik Pustakalay sewā sarvathā ni:shulka hai.

5. How many books do you lend at a time?	एक समय में आप कितनी पुस्तकें देते हैं?	Ek samay meiṅ āp kitni pustakeṅ dete haiṅ?
6. The library lends three books for fourteen days.	पुस्तकालय तीन पुस्तकें चौदह दिनों के लिए देता है।	Pustakālay tin pustakeṅ chaudah dinoṅ ke liye detā hai.
7. I see. What is the late fee per day?	अच्छा! प्रतिदिन का विलम्ब शुल्क कितना है?	Achhā, pratidin kā vilamb shulka kitnā hai.
8. We charge ten paise per day for each book.	हम प्रतिदिन प्रत्येक पुस्तक के दस पैसे लेते हैं।	Ham pratidin pratyek pustak ke das paise lete haiṅ.
9. What are the working hours of the library?	पुस्तकालय कितने बजे से कितने बजे तक खुला रहता है?	Pustakālay kitne baje se kitne baje tāk khulā rahtā hai?
10. The library remains open from 9 a.m. to 7.30 p.m.	पुस्तकालय प्रात: नौ बजे से सायं साढ़े सात बजे तक खुला रहता है।	Pustakālay prataḥ nau baje se sayam sāṛhe sāt baje tāk khulā rahtā hai.

AT THE THEATRE सिनेमा घर में

1. It's interval. Shall we go to the snack bar and have a cup of tea.	मध्यावकाश हो गया। अल्पाहार गृह चलकर एक-एक प्याला चाय ले लें?	Madhyāvkāsh ho gayā. Alpāhar girh chalkar ek-ek pyālā chay le leṅ?
2. I don't want any thing. Let us stretch our legs.	मुझे कुछ नहीं चाहिए। जरा अपनी टांगे सीधी कर लें।	Mujhe kūchh nahiṅ chāhiye. Zarā apni taṅgeṅ sidhi kar leṅ.

3.	Let us go. What do you think of heroine?	चलो चलें। नायिका के बारे में तुम्हारा क्या विचार है?	Chalo chaleṅ. Nāyikā ke bāre meiṅ tumhārā kyā vichār hai?
4.	Her performance was very good.	उसका प्रदर्शन बहुत अच्छा था।	Uskā pradarshan bahut achchhā thā.
5.	Really her future is very good.	वस्तुतः उसका भविष्य बहुत उज्ज्वल है।	Vastutaḥ uskā bhaviḥya bahut ujjval hai.
6.	She cartainly surpassed all the actors.	वह निश्चय ही सब अभिनेताओं से आगे बढ़ गई।	Vah nishchay hi sab abhinetāoṅ se age baṛh gayi.
7.	None of the others was as good as she was.	जितनी अच्छी वह रही उतना कोई दूसरा नहीं रहा।	Jitni achchhi vah rahi utnā koi dūsrā nahiṅ rahā.
8.	Except the young child Mira who made us all laugh.	केवल नन्हीं बच्ची मीरा को छोड़कर जिसने हम सबका मनोरंजन किया।	Kewel naṅhi bachchi Mira ko chhor kar, jisne ham sabhā manoranjan kiyā.
9.	The bell is ringing. It's time to go back.	घंटी बज रही है। यह लौटने का समय है।	Ghanti baj rahi hai. Yah lauṭane kā samay hai.

45TH STEP पैंतालीसवीं सीढ़ी

ASKING THE WAY
रास्ता पूछते हुए

1.	Excuse me. Can you tell me where is the temple?	आपको कष्ट न हो क्या आप बता सकते हैं कि मंदिर कहां है?	Āpko kaḥṭa nā ho to kyā āp batā saktē haiṅ ki Mandir kahāṅ hai?
2.	Which temple do you look for?	कौन सा मंदिर?	Kaunsā maṅdir?
3.	I mean the tempe of Laxmi Narayan.	मेरम मतलब है, लक्ष्मी नारायण मंदिर।	Mera matlab hai, Lakshmi Nārāyan Mandir.
4.	Oh, the Birla Mandir Go straight to the first traffic light and then turn left.	अच्छा, बिरला मंदिर। पहली ट्रैफिक बत्ती तक सीधे जाइए और फिर दायें घूमिए।	Achchhā, Birla Mandir. Pahli trafik batti tak sidhe jāiye aur phir dayeṅ ghūmiye.
5.	I see. Is it far?	अच्छा! क्या यह दूर है?	Achchhā! kyā yah dūr hai?
6.	Not so far. Only one km.	नहीं, अधिक दूर नहीं। केवल एक किलोमीटर।	Nahiṅ, adhik dūr nahiṅ. Kewel ek kilomitar.

7. Turn left at the first traffic light?	पहली ट्रैफिक बत्ती पर बायीं ओर घूमना है?	Pahli trafik batti par bayiṅ or ghūmnā hai?
8. When you turn left, you will see the temple.	जब आप बायीं ओर घूमेंगे, तो मंदिर आपको दिखाई देगा।	Jab āp bayiṅ or ghūmeṅge, to mandir āpko dikhāi degā.
9. Thanking you.	आपका धन्यवाद!	Apkā dhanyavād!
10. Not at all. It is a matter of gladness to help a stranger.	ऐसी कोई बात नहीं। अजनबी की सहायता करना प्रसन्नता की बात है।	Aisi koi bāt nahiṅ. Ajnabi ki sahāytā karnā prasannatā ki bāt hai.

AT THE MEDICAL STORE कैमिस्ट की दूकान पर

1. Can you make up this prescription for me, please?	क्या आप मेरी पर्ची की दवाई दे सकेंगे?	Kyā āp meri parchi ki dawāi de sakeṅge?
2. Certainly gentleman, will you come back later?	अवश्य, महोदय। क्या आप थोड़ी देर बाद फिर आ सकेंगे?	Avashya, mahoday! Kyā āp thoṛi der bād phir ā sakeṅge?
3. How long will it take?	कितना समय लगेगा।	Kitnā samay legegā?
4. Only ten minutes.	केवल दस मिनट।	Kewel das minat.
5. Could you recommend something for headache?	क्या आप सिरदर्द के लिए कोई दवा बताएंगे?	Kyā āp sirdard ke liya koi dawā batāyeṅge?
6. Yes, these tablets are very	हां, ये टिकिया बड़ी प्रभावपूर्ण हैं।	Hāṅ, ye tikiyāṅ baṛi prabhāvpūrṇa haiṅ.

	effective. Mostly doctors prescribe them nowadays.	आजकल बहुधा डॉक्टर इनको देते हैं।	Ajkal bahudhā dakṭar in ko dete haiṅ.
7.	All right. I will take ten tablets.	बहुत अच्छा! मैं दस टिकिया लूंगा।	Bahut achchhā. Maiṅ das tikiyāṅ lūṅgā.
8.	Will that be all, gentlemen?	इतना ही है न महोदय?	Itnā hi hai na. mahoday?
9.	Yes, except for my medicines? Will it be ready now?	जी हां, केवल मेरी पर्ची की दवाई। क्या वह अभी तैयार हो जाएगी?	Ji haṅ, kewel meri parchi ki dawāī. Kyā vah abhi taiyār ho jayegi?
10.	Not yet. Wait for a short while. Please be seated.	नहीं, अभी नहीं। थोड़ी देर प्रतीक्षा कीजिए। कृपया बैठ जाइए।	Nahiṅ, abhi nahiṅ. Thoṛi pratikṣā kijiye.Kripayā baiṭh jaiye.

ON THE TELEPHONE दूरभाष पर

1.	Is it Diamand Pocket Books?	डायमंड पॉकेट बुक्स?	Diamand paket buks?
2.	Yes, Diamand. Good morning.	जी हां, डायमंड। नमस्कार।	Ji hāṅ, Diamand. Namaskar.
3.	May I speak to Mr. Narendra Kumar?	क्या श्री नरेंद्र कुमार हैं।	Kya Shri Narendra Kumar haiṅ?
4.	Sorry, he was no arrived yet.	खेद है, वह अभी आये नहीं हैं।	Khed hai, vah abhi aye nahiṅ haiṅ.
5.	Can you tell when he will come?	क्या आप बता सकते हैं, वे कब आएंगे?	Kyā āp bata sakte haiṅ, ve kab ayeṅge?

6.	I don't know. You can give me your message.	मैं नहीं जानता। आप अपना संदेश दे सकते हैं।	Main nahiṅ jāntā. Āp apnā saṅdesh de sakte haiṅ.
7.	Will you convey him that I-Mr. Lamba called and ask him to ring me back as early as possible.	क्या आप उन्हें कह देंगे कि श्री लांबा का फोन आया था, और वे मुझे आकर जल्दी से जल्दी फोन कर लें?	Kyā āp uṅheṅ kah deṅge ki Shri Lāmbā kā phon āyā thā, aur ve mujhe ākar jaldi se jaldi phon kar leṅ?
8.	O.K. What is your telephone number please?	कह दूंगा। आपका फोन नंबर क्या है?	Kah dūṅgā. Āpkā phon number kyā hai?
9.	My number is 654527•, Mr. Narendra already knows.	मेरा नंबर 654527* है-श्री नरेंद्र कुमार इसे जानते हैं।	Merā number 654527* hai-Shri Narendra Kumar ise jante haiṅ.
10.	Very well, sir. I shall tell-him as soon as he reaches.	बहुत अच्छा, श्रीमान्! जैसे ही वह आयेंगे, मैं उन्हें बता दूँगा।	Bahut achchha, Shriman! Jaise he vah ayeṅge maiṅ unheṅ bata duṅga.
11.	Thanks. Please rememder, it is most urgent. Good bye.	धन्यवाद। कृपया ध्यान रखिए यह अत्यावश्यक है। अलविदा!	Dhanyavād! Kripayā dhyān rakhiya. Yah atyāvashyak hai. Alvidā?
	*six five four five two seven	*छः पांच चार पांच दो सात।	*Chhaḥ pāṅch chār pāṅch do sāt.

46TH STEP छियालीसवीं सीढ़ी

MAKING A TRUNK CALL
ट्रंक कॉल करते समय

Subscriber—Hello Exchange!	ग्राहक-हेलो एक्सचेंज।	Grāhak—Helo exchenj!
Operaṭor—Yes, Exchange speaking.	चालक-जी हां, एक्सचेंज से बोल रहा हूं।	Chalak—Ji hāṅ, exchenj se bol rahā hūṅ.
Subs—Please book an urgent trunk call.	ग्राहक-कृपया एक आवश्यक ट्रंक कॉल बुक कीजिए।	Grāhak—Kripayā ek āvashyak trank kāl buk kijiye.
Op—For which city?	चालक-किस शहर के लिए?	Chālak—Kis shahar ke liye.
Subs—For Pune, please.	ग्राहक-जी, पुणे के लिए।	Grāhak—Ji, Pune ke liye.
Op—What number, please.	चालक-कौन-सा नंबर?	Chālak—Kaun sā number?
Subs—6543*	ग्राहक-6543*	Grāhak—Chhaḥ pāṅch chār tin.
Op—Is the call in name of person?	चालक-क्या कॉल व्यक्तिगत है?	Chālak—Kyā kāl vyaktigat hai?
Subs—Yes, please, it is in the name of Yash Shah.	ग्राहक-हां श्रीमान् यह यश शाह के नाम से है।	Grāhak—Hāṅ shrimān, yah Yash Shah ke nām se hai.

Op—Please spell out the name.	चालक-कृपया नाम के हिज्जे बोलिए।	Chālak—Kripayā nām ke hijje boliye.
Subs—Y for Yamunanagar, A for Agra, S for Srinagar, H for Hyderabad. Deccan College, Pune.	ग्राहक-य से यमुनानगर श से शिवपुरी, य श यश शाह दक्कन कॉलेज, पुणे।	Ya se Yamunanagar, she se Shivpuri... Yash-Yash Shāh Dekkan kalej, Pune.
Op—Ok. Your phone number?	चालक-ठीक है, आपका फोन नंबर?	Chālak—ṭhik hai, āpkā phon namber?
Sub—203606+	ग्राहक-203606+	Grāhak—do shūnya tin chhaḥ shūnya chhaḥ.
Op—Well, please wait for five minutes or so.	चालक-ठीक है। पांचेक मिनट प्रतीक्षा कीजिए।	Chālak—thik hai. Pāṅchek minaṭ pratikṣa kijiye.
Subs—What is my registration number?	ग्राहक-मेरा पंजीकरण नंबर क्या है?	Grāhak—Merā paṅjikaraṇ nambar kyā hai?
Op—B for Bombay 1002×	चालक-ब से बंबई 1002×	Chālak—ba se Bambai ek shūnya shūnya do.
Subs—Thank you, Sir.	ग्राहक-धन्यवाद श्रीमान्!	Grāhak—Dhanyavād shriman!
[After seven minutes]	[सात मिनट बाद]	[Sat minat bad]

Op—Hello, is it 203606?+	चालक-हेलो! नंबर 203606?+	Chālak—Helo! nambar do shūnya tin chhaḥ shūnya chhaḥ.
Subs—Yes speaking.	ग्राहक-हां, बोल रहा हूं।	Grāhak—Hāṅ, bol rahā hūṅ.
Op—Here is your trunk call to Pune. Please speak to your person.	चालक-पुणे के लिए आपका ट्रंक कॉल ...अपने व्यक्ति से बात कीजिए।	Chalak—Pune ke liye āpkā ṭrank kāl... apne vyakti se bat kijiye.
Subs—Thank you very much.	ग्राहक-आपका बहुत धन्यवाद।	Grāhak—Apka bahut dhanyavad.
Subs—Hello, Yash Shah?	ग्राहक-हेलो, यश शाह?	Grāhak—Helo, Yash Shāh?
Yash—Speaking.	यश-बोल रही हूं।	Yash—Bol rahi hūṅ.
Subs—Amit from Delhi.	ग्राहक-दिल्ली से, अमित बोल रहा हूं।	Grāhak—Dilli se Amit bol rahā hūṅ.
Yash—Oh! Your father was much anxious about you.	यश-अच्छा! तुम्हारे पिता जी तुम्हारे बारे में बहुत चिंतित थे।	Yash—Achchhā! tumhāre pitaji tumhāre bāre meiṅ bahut chintit the.
Amit—I arrived here only yesterday.	अमित-मैं यहां कल ही पहुंचा।	Amit—Maiṅ yahāṅ kal hi pahuṅchā.
Yash—How are all in family?	यश-परिवार में सभी कैसे हैं? मेरी भाभी	Yash—Pariwar meiṅ sabhi

How is my sister-in law? your mother?	तुम्हारी माँ जी कैसी हैं।	kaise haiṅ? Mari bhābhi-tumhāri māṅji kaisi haiṅ?
Amit—All are OK. Where is my father?	अमित-सभी ठीक-ठाक हैं मेरे पिता जी कहां हैं?	Amit—Sabhi ṭhik ṭhak hai. Mere pitaji kahāṅ haiṅ?
Yash—He had gone to attend a literary meeting.	यश-वह एक साहित्य-गोष्ठी में गए हैं।	Yash—Ve ek sāhitya goṣṭhi meiṅ gaye haiṅ.
Amit—How is he?	अमित-वह कैसे हैं?	Amit—Vah kaise haiṅ?
Yash—My brother? He is very well. He is busy in compiling a classified dictionary.	यश- मेरे भाई जी? वह स्वस्थ-प्रसन्न हैं। वह एक वर्गीकृत शब्दकोश संपादित करने में व्यस्त हैं।	Yash—Mere bhai ji? Vah swastha-prasanna hai. Vah ek vargikrit shabda-kosh sampādit karne meiṅ vyasta haiṅ.
Amit—How is the uncle?	अमित-फूफाजी कैसे हैं?	Amit—Phūphāji kaise haiṅ?
Yash—Very well. To day he has gone to Bombay.	यश-वह ठीक-ठाक हैं! आज बम्बई गए हैं।	Yash—Vah ṭhik-ṭhak haiṅ. Aj Bambai gaye haiṅ.
Amit—How much work is to be done yet?	अमित-अभी काम कितना बाकी है?	Amit—Abhi kam kitnā bāki hai?

Yash—The work is almost done. Only revision is required.	यश-काम तो लगभग हो चुका है। केवल पुनरावलोकन होना है।	Yash—Kām to lagbhag ho chukā hai. Kewel punaravlokan honā hai.
Amit—Ask my father to ring me up tomorrow morning at half past six.	अमित-मेरे पिताजी से कहना कि वह मुझे कल साढ़े छः बजे फोन करें।	Amit—Mere pitāji se kahnā ki vah mujhe kal prātaḥ saṛhe chhaḥ baje phon kareṅ.
Yash—Ok. I shall convey him.	यश-ठीक है, मैं कह दूंगी।	Yash—Ṭhik hai, maiṅ kah dūṅgi.
[After concluding the talk]	(वार्ता समाप्त करते हुए)	[Vārtā samāpta karte hue]
Subs—Hello, Sir, my talk is finished. Would you kindly let me know the charges?	ग्राहक-हेलो श्रीमान्! मेरी वार्ता समाप्त हो गयी है। कृपया पैसे बताइए।	Grāhak—Helo shrimān! Meri vāṛtā samāpta ho gayi hai. Kripayā paise bataiye.
Op—Rupees Sixty, Sir.	चालक-साठ रुपये श्रीमान्।	Chalak—Saṭh rupaye shrimān!
Subs—Thank you.	ग्राहक-आपका धन्यवाद।	Grāhak—Āpkā dhanyavād!

*six five four three—छः पांच चार तीन।

+two not three six not six—दो शून्य तीन छः शून्य छः

×one not not two—एक शून्य शन्य दो।

47TH STEP सैंतालीसवीं सीढ़ी

ABOUT A TRIP
भ्रमण के बारे में

Abha—Puja, have ever been to Mahabali-puram?	आभा-पूजा, क्या तुम कभी महाबलीपुरम् गई हो?	Abha—Pūjā, kyā tum kabhi Mahābali-puram gayi ho?
Puja—No, I could not spare my time for it.	पूजा-नहीं, मैं इसके लिए कभी समय नहीं निकाल पाई।	Pūjā—Nahiṅ, maiṅ iske liye kabhi samay nahi nikāl pāyi.
Abha—Just have a short trip. It enables you to withness a charming scenery.	आभा-थोड़ा-सा घूम-घाम आओ। तुम्हें बहुत अच्छे दृश्य देखने को मिलेंगे।	Abhā—Ṭhoṛa-sa ghūm-ghām āo. Tumheṅ bahut achchhe driṣya dekhne ko mileṅge.
Puja—Ok. I shall go for a short visit tomorraw with my father.	पूजा-ठीक है, कल मैं अपने पिताजी के साथ इस लघु भ्रमण पर जाऊंगी।	Pūjā—Ṭhik hai, kal maiṅ apne pitāji ke sāth is laghu bhramaṇ par jauṅgi.
[The very next day	(दूसरे ही दिन	[Dūsre hi din. Ābhā

Abha asks Puja]	आभा पूजा से पूछती है)	Pujā se pūchhati hai]
Abha—How did you like Mahabalipuram?	आभा-तुम्हें महाबलीपुरम् कैसा लगा?	Ābhā—Tumhen Mahābalipuram kaisa legā?
Puja—It was really marvellous.	पूजा-दरअसल यह बड़ा अद्भूत था।	Pujā—Darasal yah baṛā adbhut thā.
Abha—Have you not visited the sculptures by the side of sea-shore?	आभा-समुद्रतट पर स्थित मूर्तिशिल्प को तुमने नहीं देखा क्या?	Ābhā—Samudrataṭ par sṭhit mūrtishilpa ko tum ne nahiṅ dekhā kyā?
Puja—Indeed, I have, but I am not attracted to it by some religious faith.	पूजा-सचमुच देखा है। पर मैं इसकी ओर किसी धार्मिक भावना के कारण आकृष्ट नहीं हुई।	Pujā—Sachmuch dekhā hai. Par maiṅ iski or kisi dhārmik bhāwanā ke kāran akriṣṭ nahiṅ hui.
Abha—Understand my point. You are a poet. Did you not see any work of art in the sculpture scattered around Mahabalipuram?	आभा-मेरा दृष्टिकोण समझो। तुम एक कवयित्री हो। क्या तुम महाबलीपुरम् के आस-पास फैले मूर्तिशिल्प में कला कर्म नहीं देखतीं?	Ābhā—Merā drisṭikon samjho. Tum ek kavayitri ho. Kyā tum Mahābalipuram ke āspās phaile Mūrtishilp men kala karm nahiṅ dekhtiṅ?

Puja—I here are certainly works of art and I appreciated them. I was really impressed.	पूजा-सचमुच उनमें कला कर्म है और उसकी प्रशंसक हूं। मैं सचमुच प्रभावित भी हुई।	Pūjā—Sachmuch unmeṅ kalākarm hai aur maiṅ uski prashaṅsak hūṅ. Maiṅ sachmuch prabhāvit bhi hūi.
Abha—Apart this, how did you enjoy the view of sea?	आभा-इसको छोड़ो। वैसे समुद्र के दृश्य से तुमने कितना आनंद लिया?	Ābhā—Is ko chhoro. Vaise samundra ke driṣya se tumne kitnā ānand liyā?
Puja—I cannot express that in words. It was marvellous indeed!	पूजा-मैं शब्दों में अभिव्यक्त नहीं कर सकती। वास्तव में यह अद्भुत था।	Pūjā—Maiṅ shabdoṅ meiṅ abhivyakta nahiṅ kar sakti. Vāstav meiṅ yah adbhut thā.

ABOUT A TOUR
यात्रा के बारे में

Uma—Papa, you are coming back after two months. Please tell me, what places you have visited.	उमा-पिताजी, आप दो मास बाद लौटे हैं। बताइए न, आपने कौन-से स्थान देखे।	Umā—Pitāji ap do mās bād laute haiṅ. Batāiya nā, āpne kaun se sthān dekhe?

Papa—Come on my daugher. I am returning after touring throughout India.	पिता-आओ मेरी बेटी। मैं भारत-भर भ्रमण करके लौटा हूं।	Pitā—Āo meri beti Main Bhārat-bhar bhramaṇ karke lauṭa hūṅ.
Uma—Papa, where did you go first?	उमा-पिताजी, पहले आप कहां गए?	Umā—Pitāji pahle āp kahaṅ gaye?
Papa—First of all, I went to Delhi. Delhi is the Captial of India.	पिता-सबसे पहले मैं दिल्ली गया। दिल्ली भारत की राजधानी है।	Pita—Sabse pahle main Dilli gayā. Dilli Bhārat ki rājdhani hai.
Uma—What did you see in Delhi?	उमा-आपने दिल्ली में क्या देखा?	Umā—Āpne Dilli meiṅ kyā dekhā?
Papa—In Old Delhi. I saw the Red Fort. I visited the Central Secretariate, the Birla Mandir and the Qutub Minar in New Delhi.	पिता-मैंने पुरानी दिल्ली में लाल-किला देखा। नई दिल्ली में केंद्रीय सचिवालय, बिरला मंदिर और कुतुब मीनार देखे।	Pita—Maiṅ ne purāni Dilli meiṅ Lal Kila dekhā. Nai Dilli meiṅ Kendriya Sachivālaya, Birlā Mandir aur Kutab Minār dekhe.
Uma—Where did you go afterward?	उमा-उसके बाद आप कहां गए?	Umā—Uske bād āp kahaṅ gaye?
Papa—After that	पिता-फिर मैं बम्बई	Pita—Phir maiṅ

I went to Bombay. Bombay is the biggest port of India.	गया। बम्बई भारत की सबसे बड़ी बंदरगाह है।	Bambai gayā. Bambai Bhārat ki sabse bari bandargāh hai.
Uma—Then you must have witnessed the sea and big ships also.	उमा-तब तो आपने समुद्र और बड़े-बड़े जहाज देखे होंगे।	Umā—Tab to āpne samudra aur baṛe-baṛe jahāz bhi dekhe hoṅge.
Papa—Yes, I have seen many ships.	पिता-हां, मैंने बहुत जलयान देखे।	Pitā—Hāṅ maiṅ ne bahut jalyān dekhe.
Uma—Papa did you not go to Agra?	उमा-पिताजी, आप आगरा नहीं गए क्या?	Umā—Pitāji āp Āgra nahiṅ gaye kyā?
Papa—Oh yes, I went to Agra also and visited the Taj, and dropped at Mathura too, for a day.	पिता-अरे हाँ, मैं आगरा भी गया ताज देखा और एक दिन के लिए मथुरा भी रुका?	Pitā—Are hāṅ, maiṅ Āgrā bhi gayā, Tāj dekha aur ek din ke liye Mathurā bhi rukā.
Uma—Will you please point out on the map the places you visited papa?	उमा-पिताजी, क्या आप मानचित्र पर उन स्थानों को दिखा सकते हैं जो अपने देखे हैं?	Umā—Pitāji, kyā āp mānchitra par un sthānoṅ ko dikhā sakte haiṅ jo āpne dekhe haiṅ?
Papa—Why not my child, come with map. I will	पिता-क्यों नहीं मेरी बेटी अपना मानचित्र लाओ। मैं तुम्हें	Pitā—Kyoṅ nahiṅ meri beti, apnā mānchitra lāo.

show you everything.	सब कुछ दिखाऊंगा।	Maiṅ tumheṅ sabkuchh dikhāuṅgā.
Uma—Thank you Papa, I am coming with classmate Satyakam.	उमा-धन्यवाद पिताजी, मैं अपने सहपाठी सत्यकाम के साथ आ रही हूं।	Umā—Dhanyavād pitāji, maiṅ apne sahpāṭhi Satyakām ke sāth ā rahi hūṅ.
Papa—O.K. my child.	पिता-ठीक है, आओ मेरी बिटिया।	Pitā—Ṭhik hai, āo meri biṭiyā.

•••

48TH STEP अड़तालीसवीं सीढ़ी

THE VILLAGER & THE URBN

ग्रामीण और शहरी

Urban—How are you! I am seeing you after a very ḷong time.	शहरी-आप कैसे हैं! मैं आपको बहुत दिनों बाद देख रहा हूं।	Shahri—Āp kaise haiṅ! Maiṅ āpko bahut dinoṅ bād dekh rahā hūṅ.
Villager—Yes friend, I have come here on a particular business and will return back this night.	ग्रामीण-हां मित्र, मैं यहां एक विशेष काम से आया हूं और इसी रात को वापस लौट जाऊंगा।	Grāmiṇ—Hāṅ Mitra, maiṅ yahāṅ ek vishes kām se āyā hūṅ aur isi rāt ko vāpas laut jaūṅga.
Urban—Why so soon? Do you hesitate to stay in towns?	शहरी-इतनी जल्दी क्यों? क्या आप शहरों में रहने से हिचकते हैं?	Shahri—Itni jaldi kyoṅ? Kyā āp shahroṅ meiṅ rahne se hichakte haiṅ?
Villager—Yes gentleman, I	ग्रामीण-हां महाशय, मुझे कतई पसंद	Grāmiṇ—Hāṅ Mahāshay,

don't like town at all. I do not find any pleasure in the filthy atmosphere of the towns-hustle and bustle irritates me.	नहीं। मुझे शहर के गंदे वातावरण में कुछ मजा नहीं आता-भीड़भाड़ से मैं बौखला उठता हूं।	mujhe shahar ke gaṅde vātāvaraṇ meiṅ kuchh majā nahiṅ ātā. Bhiṛ-bhaṛ se maiṅ baukhalā uṭhta hāṅ.
Urban—Wonder! How can you enjoy life without hustle and bustle? I would not bear the calmness and silence of the village. It would make me mad.	शहरी-आश्चर्य! आप भीड़-भाड़ के बिना जीवन का आनंद कैसे लेते हैं? मैं तो गांव की शांति और चुप्पी को बर्दाश्त ही न कर पाऊंगा। उससे मैं पागल हो उठूँगा।	Shahri—Āschary! Ap bhiṛ-bhāṛ ke binā jivan kā ānaṅd kaise lete haiṅ? Maiṅ to gaon ki shāṅti aur chuppi ko bardāsht hi na kar paūṅgā. Usase maiṅ pāgal ho uṭhūṅgā.
Villager—Everyman has his own attitude, but I much love the rural beauty.	ग्रामीण-हर व्यक्ति का अपना दृष्टिकोण होता है। पर मैं ग्रामीण सौंदर्य को अधिक प्यार करता हूं।	Grāmiṇ—Har vvakti kā apnā drishtikoṇ hotā hai. Par maiṅ grāmiṇ saundarya ko adhik pyar karta hūṅ.
Urban—Are you getting something of this modern age in your village?	शहरी-क्या आप इस आधुनिक युग का कुछ भी अपने गांव में पाते हैं?	Shahri—Kyā āp is ādhunik yug kā kuchh bhi apne gāoṅ meiṅ pāte haiṅ?
Villager—The thing which	ग्रामीण-जो चीज गांव में मिल सकती है	Grāmiṇ—Jo chiz gāoṅ meiṅ mil

can be gotten in the village can never be gotten in the town.	वह शहर में कदापि नहीं।	sakti hai vah shahar meiṅ kadāpi nahiṅ!
Urban—Oh! Do you want to live in quite atmosphere alone? Will your life not be dull without cinema, sports and other social activities?	शहरी–ओह! क्या आप वातावरण में अकेले रहना चाहते हैं? आप का जीवन सिनेमा, खेलकूद और दूसरी सामाजिक गतिविधियों के बिना नीरस नहीं हो जाएगा?	Shahri—Kyā āp shāṅt vatāvaraṇ meiṅ akele rahnā chāhte haiṅ? Āpkā jivan sinema, khelkūd aur dusri sāmājik gatividhioṅ ke bina niras nahiṅ ho jāyegā?
Villager—I think that will be much better. Of course the town had made the human life a machine.	ग्रामीण–मेरा विचार है, वह अपेक्षाकृत अच्छा रहेगा। निःसंदेह शहर ने मानव जीवन को मशीन बनाकर रख दिया है।	Grāmiṇ—Merā vichār hai, vah apekṣakrit achchhā rahega. Ni:-saṅdeh shahar ne mānav-jiwan ko mashin banakar rakh diyā hai.
Urban—But can a nation prosper without its great cities?	शहरी–परंतु क्या कोई राष्ट्र बिना अपने बड़े शहरों के फल-फुल सकता है?	Shahri—Paraṅtu kyā koi rāshtra binā apne baṛe shaharoṅ ke fal-fūl sakta hai.
Villager—But never forget that the foundation of	ग्रामीण–पर यह मत भूलिए कि हमारे राष्ट्र की नींव हमारे गांवों पर	Grāmiṇ—Par yah mat bhūliye ki hamāre rāshtra ki niṅv hamāre

our nation really lies on its village. Without the improvement of the village, the nation cannot. progress.	टिकी है। गांवों की दशा सुधारे बिना राष्ट्र उन्नति नहीं कर सकता।	gāvoṅ par tiki hai. Gāvoṅ ki dasha sudhāre binā rashtra unnati nahiṅ kar saktā.
Urban—I admit it, but I don't think of leaving the cities.	शहरी-मैं इसे स्वीकार करता हूं पर मैं शहर को छोड़ने की बात नहीं सोच सकता।	Shahri—Maiṅ ise swikār kartā hūṅ par maiṅ shahra ko chhoṛne ki bāt nahiṅ soch saktā.
Villager—Thank you for the good talk. Now I am in a hurry. We shall talk again whenever we find time. Good bye.	ग्रामीण-अच्छी बातचीत के लिए आपका धन्यवाद! अब मैं थोड़ा जल्दी में हूं। जब भी समय मिलेगा, हम फिर बात करेंगे। अच्छा चलता हूं।	Grāmiṇ—Achchhi batchit ke liye āpkā dhanya-wād. Ab maiṅ thoṛhā jaldi meiṅ hūṅ. Jab bhi samay milegā, ham phir bat karenge. Achchā chaltā hūṅ.
Urban—Bye-bye. See you again.	शहरी-अच्छा विदा! फिर मिलेंगे।	Shahri—Achchhā vidā! Phir mileṅge.

•••

49TH STEP उनचासवीं सीढ़ी

THE DOCTOR & THE PATIENT
डॉक्टर और रोगी

Patient—Good morning, doctor! Can you spare for me a few minutes?	रोगी-नमस्कार डॉक्टर साहब! क्या आप कुछ मिनट मुझे दे सकेंगे?	Rogi—Namaskār Dāktar sahab! Kyā āp kuchh minaṭ mujhe de sakeṅge?
Doctor—Who not? Take seat... Now, tell me what is wrong with you?	डॉक्टर-क्यों नहीं? बैठिए...अब बताइए, आपको क्या हुआ है?	Dāktor—Kyoṅ nahiṅ? Baithiye...ab baṭāiye, āpko kyaā huā hai?
Patient—I have lost my appetite. I am always suffering from indigestion. And what is worse, I cannot sleep well at night.	रोगी-मेरी भूख मर गई है। मैं हर समय बदहजमी से ग्रस्त रहता हूं। और सबसे खराब बात यह है कि मैं रात को सो नहीं पाता।	Rogi—Meri bhūkh mār gayi hai. Maiṅ har samay badhazmi se grast rahtā hūṅ. Aur sabse kharāb bāt yah hai ki maiṅ rāt ko so nahiṅ pātā.

Doctor—I see. What are you?	डॉक्टर-ओह, यह बात है। आप करते क्या हैं?	Daktar—Oh, yah bāt hai. Āp karte kyā haiṅ?
Patient—I am a senior proof reader in a well established printing press. I have to work long hours on my seat.	रोगी-मैं प्रवर प्रूफ संशोधक हूं- एक प्रतिष्ठित छपाई खाने में। मुझे अपनी कुर्सी पर घंटों तक काम करना पड़ता है।	Rogi—Maiṅ prawar prūf saṅshodhak hūṅ–ek pratiṣhṭhit chhāpāikhāne meiṅ. Mujhe apni kursi par ghaṅtoṅ ṭak kām karnā paṛtā hai.
Doctor—Are you habitual of evening walk?	डॉक्टर-क्या आप शाम की सैर के अभ्यस्त हैं?	Dāktar—Kyā āp shām ki sair ke abhyast haiṅ?
Patient—No doctor, I do not go for a walk in the evening. I feel too much tired when I get home, I simply take my food and go to bed.	रोगी-नहीं डॉक्टर साहब! मैं शाम को सैर नहीं करता। जब मैं घर, पहुंचता हूं तो मैं बड़ा थका महसूस करता हूं। बस, मैं खाना खाता हूं और लेट जाता हूं।	Rogi—Nahiṅ Dāktar sahab! Maiṅ shām ko sair nahiṅ kartā. Jab maiṅ ghar panūṅchtā hūṅ to maiṅ baṛā ṭhakā mahasūs kartā hūṅ. Bus maiṅ khānā khātā hūṅ aur so jātā hūṅ.
Doctor—As I	डॉक्टर-मेरे विचार से,	Daktar—Mere

think, your troubles are due to your indisciplined life. Take rest and do proper physical labour.	तुम्हारी परेशानियों की जड़ तुम्हारा अस्त व्यस्त जीवन ही है। आराम कर और नियमित शारीरिक श्रम करो।	vichār se, thmhāri pareshaniyoṅ ki jarh tumhārā ast-vyast jiwan hi hai. Ārām karo aur niyamit shāaririk shram karo.
Patient—I agree you. I could not get any leave for a long time.	रोगी–मैं आपसे सहमत हूं। मैं लम्बे समय से कोई अवकाश नहीं पा सका।	Rogi—Maiṅ āpse sahmat hūṅ. Maiṅ lambe samay se koi awakāsh nahiṅ pā sakā.
Doctor—Well. I advise you to any country-side for some days. Rest in the open air, keeping the doors open. Take walk in the morning and the evening. Improve your diet. Be regular in rest and sleep. I think, by following these instructions	डॉक्टर–अच्छा तो मैं आपको सलाह दूंगा कि आप कुछ समय के लिए ग्रामीण क्षेत्र में जाएं। दरवाजे खुले रखकर खुली हवा में आराम करें सुबह–शाम सैर करें। अपनी खुराक ठीक करावें। आराम और विश्राम में नियमित बनें। मैं समझता हूं इन निर्देशों को अपनाकर आप थोड़े समय में ही बिल्कुल स्वस्थ हो जाएंगे।	Dāktar—Achchhā to main apko salāh dūṅgā ki āp kuchh samay ke liye grāmiṇ kṣetra meiṅ jayeṅ. Darwāze khule rakhkar khuli hawa meiṅ ārām kareṅ. Subah-shām sair kareṅ. Apni khūrāk ṭhik kareṅ. Ārām aur vishrām meiṅ

you will be allright in very short period.		niyamit beneṅ. Maiṅ samajhatā hūṅ in nirdeshoṅ ko apnākar āp thore samay meiṅ hi bilkul swastha ho jayeṅge.
Patient—Thank you, doctor! I shall follow your instructions positively. Thanks!	रोगी-धन्यवाद, डॉक्टर! मैं आपके निर्देशों का अवश्य पालन करूँगा। धन्यवाद!	Rogi—Dhanyavād Dāktar! Maiṅ āpke nirdeshoṅ kā awashya pālan kurūṅgā! Dhanyawād!
Doctor—Please visit me after ten days. I think you will improve.	डॉक्टर-दस दिनों बाद आइएगा। मेरा विचार है, आपके स्वास्थ्य में सुधार होगा।	Dāktar—Das dinoṅ bād ayegā Merā wichār hai, āpke swāsthya meiṅ sudhār hogā.

•••

50TH STEP पचासवीं सीढ़ी

SELF-INTRODUCTION
आत्मपरिचय

1. My name is Shahnaz	मेरा नाम शहनाज	Merā nām Shanāz hai.
2. I am an Indian and live in Pune.	मैं भारतीय हूँ और पुणे में रहती हूँ।	Main bhārtiya hūṅ aur Pune meiṅ rahati hūṅ.
3. I have just completed.	मैं सत्रह वर्ष की हूँ।	Maiṅ satrah varṣha ki hūṅ.
4. I am a virgin.	मैं कुमारी हूँ।	Maiṅ kumāri hūṅ.
5. I am a student and studying in 10th class.	मैं छात्रा हूँ और दसवीं कक्षा में पढ़ती हूँ।	Maiṅ chhatrā hūṅ aur dasaviṅ kakṣā meiṅ paṛhti hūṅ.
6. My father is senior officer in P.M.T.	मेरे पिताजी पी. एम. टी. में वरिष्ठ अधिकारी है।	Mere Pitāji pi.em.ti. meiṅ varisṭh adhi-kāri haiṅ.
7. I have to brothers and three sisters.	मेरे दो भाई और तीन बहनें हैं।	Mere do bhāi aur tin bahneṅ haiṅ.
8. My elder brother is an engineer.	मेरे भाईसाहब अभियन्ता हैं।	Mere bhāisāhab abhiyaṅtā haiṅ.
9. My younger	मेरे छोटा भाई	Mere chhotā bhāi

	brother is kind hearted.	दयालु हृदय है।	dayalu-hriday hai.
10.	Minaz, Gulnar and Dilshad are my younger sisters.	मीनाज, गुलनार और दिलशाद मेरी छोटी बहनें हैं।	Mināz, Gulnār aur Dilshād meri chhoti bahneṅ haiṅ.
11.	They are more intelligent than me.	वे मुझसे अधिक अक्लमंद हैं।	Ve mujhse adhik akalmaṅd haiṅ.
12.	My aim in life is to be a Scientist.	मेरे जीवन का उद्देश्य वैज्ञानिक बनना है।	Mere jiwan ka uddeshya Vaigyānik banana hai.
13.	I go to school by bicycle.	मैं विद्यालय साइकिल पर जाती हूं।	Maiṅ vidyālay saikal par jati hūṅ.
14.	I get up somewhat late in the morning	मैं प्रातः कुछ देर से उठती हूं।	Maiṅ prāta: kuchh der se uṭhti hūṅ.
15.	I know, this is bad habit.	मैं जानती हूँ, यह बुरी आदत है।	Maiṅ janti hūṅ, yah buri ādat hai.
16.	I am ashamed of it.	इसके लिए मैं लज्जित हूं।	Iske liye maiṅ lajjit hūṅ.
17.	Really, I am halpless.	वास्तव में, मैं असहाय हूं।	Vāstav meiṅ, maiṅ asahāy hūṅ.
18.	I intend to improve my habit.	मैं अपनी आदत सुधारना चाहती हूं।	Maiṅ apni ādat sudharnā chāhati hūṅ.
19.	I hope, I will overpower it.	मुझे आशा है, मैं इसे सुधार लूँगी।	Mujhe āshā hai, maiṅ ise sudhār lūṅgi.
20.	I seek the help of my family members to eradicate this evil.	इस बुरी आदत को दूर करने के लिए मैं अपने परिवार के सदस्यों की सहायता चाहती हूं।	Is buri ādat ko dūr karne ke liya maiṅ apne pariwar ke sadasyoṅ ki sahāyatā chahti hūṅ.

21. I take bath and thank God for his grace.	मैं स्नान करती हूं और खुदा की कृपा के लिए उसका धन्यवाद करती हूं।	Maiṅ snān karti hūṅ aur khuḍa ki kirpā ke liye uskā dhanyawād karti hūṅ.
22. I have some pen friends too.	मेरे कुछ पत्र-मित्र भी है।	Mere kuchh patra-mitra bhi haiṅ.
23. I write them now and then.	मैं उन्हें जब-तब (पत्र) लिखती हूं।	Maiṅ unheṅ jab-tab (patra) likhti hūṅ.
24. I respect my elders and love my youngers.	मैं बड़ों का आदर करती हूं और छोटों से प्यार।	Maiṅ baṛoṅ kā ādar karti hūṅ aur chhotoṅ se pyār.
25. My mother-tongue is Marathi, but I know Hindi also.	मेरी मातृभाषा मराठी है परंतु मैं हिंदी भी जानती हूं।	Meri mātribhāshā Marāṭhi hai paraṅtu maiṅ Hindi bhi jānti hūṅ.
26. I shall stay in Delhi for two days more.	मैं दिल्ली में दो दिन और रुकूंगी।	Maiṅ Dilli meiṅ do din aur rukūṅgi.
27. I will visit Red Fort, Qutab Minar, Jama Masjid, Dargah-e-Niza-muddin and Birla Mandir.	मैं लाल किला, कुतुब मीनार, जामा मस्जिद, निजामुद्दीन दरगाह और बिरला मंदिर जाऊंगी।	Maiṅ lāl kilā, kutub minār, jāma masjid, nizamuddin dargāh aur birla mandir jaūṅgi.
28. First of all. I am an Indian. I love all my countrymen.	सबसे पहले मैं भारतीय हूं। मैं अपने सभी देश-वासी से प्यार करती हूं।	Sabse pahle maiṅ bhārtiy hūṅ. Maiṅ apne sabhi desh-vāsiyoṅ se payār karti hūṅ.
29. I want to be a	मैं अपने देश के	Maiṅ apne desh ke

	useful citizen for nation.	लिए एक लाभ-दायक नागरिक बनना चाहती हूं।	liya ek lābhdāyak nāgrik bananā chahti hūṅ.
30.	I shall go to England for further studies this year.	मैं इस वर्ष पढ़ाई के लिए इंग्लैंड जाऊंगी।	Main is vars paṛhāi ke liya Englaṇd jaūṅgi.
31.	I don't believe in formality.	मैं तकल्लुफ में विश्वास नहीं रखती।	Maiṅ takalluf meiṅ viswās nahiṅ rakhti.
32.	I cordially thank you very much for your hospitality.	आपके आतिथ्य के लिए मैं आपका हृदय से धन्यवाद करती हूं।	Āpke ātithya ke liya mai āpkā hriday se dhanyavād karti hūṅ.
33.	Finally, hope you will overlook my faults.	अंततः मुझे विश्वास है कि आप मेरी त्रुटियों को क्षमा करेंगे।	Antat:, mujhe vishvās hai ki āp meri trutiyoṅ ko kṣamā kereṅge.
34.	I wish to be always sincere to everyone.	मैं सदा हरेक के प्रति ईमानदार बनी रहना चाहती हूं।	Maiṅ sadā harek ke prati imāndār bani rahanā chāhti hūṅ.

•••

APPENDIX

परिशिष्ट

IDIOMS & PROVERS
मुहावरे एवं लोकोक्तियाँ

IDIOMS मुहावरे

1. अंधे की लाठी — Aṅdhe ki lāṭhi — The only support.

   प्रयोग–बूढ़े माता-पिता के लिए उनका लड़का ही अंधे की लाठी है।

2. अक्ल का दुश्मन — Akla ka dushman — Idiot.

   प्रयोग– वह तो अक्ल का दुश्मन है, उससे कुछ आशा न रखो।

3. अक्ल पर पत्थर पड़ना — Akla par patthar paṛnā — To be befooled.

   प्रयोग– सुरेश की अक्ल पर पत्थर पड़ा है तभी तो उसने अपना सब कुछ खो दिया।

4. अपने मुंह मियां मिट्ठु बनाना — Apne muṅh miyāṅ miṭṭhu bananā — To do self-praise.

   प्रयोग– कुछ करोगे भी या यों ही अपने मुंह मिया मिट्ठू बनते रहोगे।

5. आंखें बिछाना — Ankhe bichhānā — To given warm welcome.

   प्रयोग–दूल्हे के स्वागत में लोग आंखें बिछाए खड़े थे।

6. आंख का तारा — Aṅkh kā tārā — Very lovely.

   प्रयोग–बच्चे अपने माता-पिता की आंख का तारा होते हैं।

7. आंख की किरकिरी — Āṅkh ki kirkiri — Eye-sore

8.	आकाश-पाताल एक करना	Ākāsh pātāl ek karna	A world a difference.

प्रयोग-दोनों भाइयों की प्रकृति में आकाश-पाताल का अंतर है।

9.	आस्तीन का सांप	Āstin ka sāṅp	A wolf in sheep's clothing.

प्रयोग- रवि तो बिल्कुल आस्तीन के सांप की तरह है, उससे दूर ही रहना अच्छा है।

10.	ईंट से ईंट बजाना	Iṅṭ se iṅṭ bajānā	To destroy completely

प्रयोग- वीर हनुमान ने लंका की ईंट से ईंट बजा दी।

11.	ईंद का चांद	Īd kā chānd	Rare visits

प्रयोग- देवेन्द्र तुम तो ईद के चांद हो गए हो। कहां रहते हो आजकल?

12.	उंगली उठाना	Uṅgli uṭhānā	To find fault

प्रयोग- चरित्रहीन व्यक्ति की ओर सभी उंगली उठाते हैं।

13.	उलटी गंगा बहाना	Ulti gaṅgā bahānā	To carry coal to new castle

प्रयोग- यदि ऐसे ही उलटी गंगा बहाओगे तो सफलता तुमसे दूर ही रहेगी।

14.	उन्नीस-बीस का अंतर	Unnis bis kā antar	A little difference

प्रयोग- दोनों मित्रों के स्वभाव में उन्नीस-बीस का अंतर है।

15.	एक ही लाठी से हांकना	Ek hi laṭhi se hāṅkanā	To treat good and bad in the same way.

प्रयोग- सब को एक ही लाठी से हांकने की नीति ठीक नहीं।

16.	एड़ी चोटी का ज़ोर लगाना	Eri choṭi kā zor lagānā	To work hard

प्रयोग- रमेश तो चुनाव जीतने के लिए एड़ी चोटी का जोर लगाया, फिर भी असफल रहा।

17. काठ का उल्लू — Kāṭh kā ullū — Dummy

प्रयोग- उस पर उचित काम की आशा मत रखो, वह तो काठ का उल्लू है।

18. खालाजी का घर — Khālāji kā ghar — An easy job.

प्रयोग- सैनिक जीवन बिताना खालाजी का घर नहीं है।

19. खेत रहना — Khet rahnā — To die in the battle field.

प्रयोग- अनेक सैनिक मातृभूमि की रक्षा के लिए खेत रहे।

20. गड़े मुर्दे उखाड़ना — Gare murde ukhāṛna — To rip up old sores.

प्रयोग- गड़े मुर्दे उखाड़ने से क्या लाभ! बीती बातों को भूल जाना चाहिए।

21. घी के दिये जलाना — Ghi ke diya jalānā — To show great pleasure.

प्रयोग- कुख्यात डाकू के मारे जाने पर गांववासियों ने घरों में घी के दिये जलाए।

22. घाव पर नमक छिड़कना — Ghāv par namak chhiṛaknā — To add injuries to the wounds.

प्रयोग- मैं पहले ही बहुत सताया गया हूं और अब तुम मेरे घावों पर नमक छिड़क रहे हो!

23. चम्पत होना — Chaṃpt honā — To take to one's heels.

प्रयोग- पुलिस के आते ही चोर वहां से चम्पत हो गया।

24. चल बसना — Chal basnā — To die

प्रयोग- राजा दशरथ पुरुषोत्तम राम के वियोग में चल बसे।

25. चिकनी-चुपड़ी बातें करना — Chikni-chupṛi bāteṅ karnā — To flatter

प्रयोग- चिकनी-चुपड़ी बातें करके अध्यक्ष ने विपक्षी नेताओं को फंसाने की कोशिश की।

26. छक्के छुड़ाना — Chhakke chhuṛānā — To force out of gear

प्रयोग- युद्ध में भारतीय सेना ने पाकिस्तानी सेना के छक्के छुड़ा दिए।

27. छाती से लगाना — Chhāti se lagānā — To embrace

प्रयोग- मां ने अपने वर्षों से बिछड़े बेटे को छाती से लगा लिया।

28. जाल बिछाना — Jāl bichchānā — To dig a pit.

प्रयोग- मोहन ने अमित को फंसाने के लिए अपने कुचक्रों का जाल फैलाया।

29. जी का बोझ हलका होना — Ji kā bojh halkā honā — Halka hona

प्रयोग- माता-पिता के बेटी की कुशलता का समाचार सुना तो उनके जी का बोझ हलका हो गया।

30. जी-जान लड़ाना — Ji-jān laṛanā — To try one's level best

प्रयोग- सेना को सामना करने के लिए जी जान लड़ाकर तैयारी करनी होगी।

31. जीना दूभर होना — Jina dūbhar honā — To live in difficuulty

प्रयोग- इस महंगाई के जमाते में गरीब व्यक्ति का जीना दूभर हो गया है।

32. जूतियां चटखाते फिरना — Jutiyāṅ chaṭkhate phirnā — To roam aimlessly.

प्रयोग- कोई ढंग का काम करो, इस तरह आखिर कब तक जूतियां चटखाते फिरोगे।

33. जलती आग में घी डालना — Jalti āg meṅ ghi dālnā — To add fuel to the flames.

प्रयोग- वह पहले से गुस्से से भरा पड़ा था, तुम्हारी बातों ने जलती आग में घी डालने का काम किया।

34. टका सा जवाब देना — Takā-sā javāb dena — To give a flat denial

प्रयोग- राकेश ने उससे सहायता मांगी लेकिन उसने टका सा जवाब दे दिया।

35.	टांग तले से निकलना	Taṅg tale se nikalnā	To acknowledge defeat

प्रयोग- आखिर अंग्रेजों को टांग तले से निकलना पड़ा।

36.	तारे गिनना	Tāre ginanā	To be anxiety.

प्रयोग- हरीश चिंता और परेशानी के कारण सारी रात तारे गिनता रहा।

37.	दम तोड़ना	Dam toṛnā	To die

प्रयोग- डॉक्टर के पहुंचने से पहले ही रोगी ने दम तोड़ दिया।

38.	दाल में काला होना	Dal meṅ kalā honā	To be something wrong at the bottom

प्रयोग- वायदा करके भी वह न पहुंची तो मैं समझ गया दाल में कुछ काला है।

39.	दुम दबाकर भागना	Dum dabākar bhāgnā	To show clean pair of heels.

प्रयोग- लड़ाई के मैदान से शत्रु दुम दबाकर भाग निकले।

40.	दौड़-धूप करना	Daur-dhūp karna	To run about.

प्रयोग- कृष्ण ने बहन के विवाह के लिए उपयुक्त वर के लिए बहुत दौड़-धूप की।

41.	दिन दुनी रात चौगुनी	Din dūni rāt chauguni	By leaps and bounds.

प्रयोग- मनोज दिन दुनी रात चौगुनी प्रगति कर रहा है।

42.	दांत खट्टे करना	Dāṅt khaṭṭe karnā	To vanquish

प्रयोग- चन्द्रशेखर आजाद ने अंग्रेजों के दांत खट्टे कर दिए थे।

43.	धूल में मिलाना	Dhūl meṅ milanā	To ruin.

प्रयोग- सुरेन्द्र ने माता-पिता की आशाओं को धूल में मिला दिया।

44.	नौ दो ग्यारह होना	Nau do gyārah hona	To run away

प्रयोग- जेब काटकर जेबकतरा नौ दो ग्यारह हो गया।

45.	नमक-मिर्च लगाना	Namak-mircha lagānā	To exaggerate a thing

प्रयोग- कुछ औरतें आपस में दूसरों की बातों को नमक-मिर्च लगाकर कहती हैं।

46. नींद हराम होना   Nind harām honā   To get no sleep
प्रयोग- बेटी के विवाह की चिंता के कारण माता-पिता की नींद हराम हो गई है।

47. पगड़ी उछालना   Pagaṛi uchhālnā   To insult
प्रयोग- हमें किसी की पगड़ी उछालने का अधिकार नहीं है।

48. परदा उठाना   Pardā uṭhānā   To reveal a secret
प्रयोग-उस व्यक्ति ने समय रहते परदा उठा दिया, नहीं तो निर्दोष मारा जाता।

49. परदा डालना   Pardā dālnā   To conceal
प्रयोग- राम ने वर्षों तक इस पर परदा डाले रखा।

50. पानी-पानी होना   Pāni-pāni hona   To be much askamed
प्रयोग-अनिल के दुर्व्यसनों की चर्चा सुनकर उसका पिता पानी-पानी हो गया।

51. पानी फेरना   Pāni pherna   To destroy
प्रयोग- कुसंगति में पड़कर पुत्र ने माता-पिता की आशाओं पर पानी फेर दिया।

52. फूट-फूटकर रोना   Phūt-phūṭkar ronā   To weep bittely
प्रयोग-जवान बेटे की आकस्मिक मृत्यु का समाचार सुनकर मां फुट-फूटकर रोने लगी।

53. फूले न समाना   Phūle nā samānā   To be over joyed
प्रयोग-बेटे की महान सफलता पर माता-पिता फूले नहीं समा रहे थे।

54. बाल-बाल बचना   Bāl bāl bachnā   A narrow escape
प्रयोग-कार दुर्घटना में वह बाल-बाल बच गया।

55. बाट जोहना   Bāṭ johnā   To wait
प्रयोग-देर रात तक पत्नी अपने पति की बाट जोहती रही।

56. मतलबी यार   Matlabi yār   Fair weather friend
प्रयोग-तुम मतलबी यार को पहचान लो। सच्चे मित्र मिलना कठिन है।

57. मारे-मारे फिरना — Māre-māre phirna — To roam about

प्रयोग-रमा नौकरी की तलाश में मारे-मारे फिर रही है।

58. मुंह में पानी भर आना — Muṅh meṅ pāni bhar ānā — To feel much greedy

प्रयोग- अंगूरों के गुच्छे देखकर लोमड़ी के मुंह में पानी भर आया।

59. मक्खियाँ मारना — Makkhiyāṅ marnā — To remain idle

प्रयोग- नौकरी के अभाव में नवयुवक मक्खियाँ मारते फिरते हैं।

60. मन के लड्डू पकाना — Man ke laddū pakānā — To make castle in the air

प्रयोग- कोई अच्छा काम कर दिखाओ, मन के लड्डू पकाने का क्या लाभ।

61. मुंह में पानी भर आना — Muṅh meṅ pāni bhar ānā — The watering of mouth

प्रयोग-लटकते हुए अंगूरों के गुच्छों को देखकर लोमड़ी के मुंह में पानी भर आया।

62. रफू-चक्कर होना — Rafn̈-chakkar hona — To run away

प्रयोग-जेबकतरा पुलिस को देखते ही रफू-चक्कर हो गया।

63. राई का पहाड़ बनाना — Rāi kā pahār banānā — To make a mountain of a mole hill

प्रयोग-तुम भी उसकी बातों में आ गई, उसे तो राई का पहाड़ बनाने की आदत है।

64. लोहा मानना — Lohā mānanā supremacy — to acknowledge

प्रयोग- आस-पास के सब राजा सम्राट् का लोहा मानते थे।

65. वचन देना — Vachan denā — To promise

प्रयोग- उसने मुझे वचन दिया था कि वह सदा मेरे साथ रहेगा।

66. शेखी मारना — Shekhi mārnā — To talk big

प्रयोग–वह अपने आपको बड़ा समझता है, हर समय शेखी मारता रहता है।

67. सामना करना — Sāmnā karnā — To face

प्रयोग– मैं हर मुसीबत का बड़े धैर्य से सामना करता हूं।

68. सर्वे-सर्वा होना — Sarve-sarvā honā — To be all in all

प्रयोग–श्री विश्वनाथ इस संस्था के सर्वेसर्वा हैं।

69. सिर पर पांव रखकर भागना — Sir par pūṅv rakhkar bhāgnā — to take to one's heels

प्रयोग–सभी जुआरी पुलिस को आते देख सिर पर पांव रखकर भाग गए।

70. हथियार डाल देना — Hathiār dal denā — To surrrender

प्रयोग– डाकुओं ने पुलिस के आगे हथियार डाल दिए।

71. हाथ पर हाथ धरे बैठना — Hāth par hāth dhare baiṭhnā — To sit idle

प्रयोग– इस तरह हाथ पर हाथ धरे कब तक बैठे रहोगे। कुछ काम-धंधा ही कर लो।

72. हाथ-पांव मारना — Hāth pāṅv mārnā — To make efforts.

प्रयोग– हमने तुम्हें पाने के लिए खूब हाथ-पांव मारे।

73. हाथ धो बैठना — Hāth dho baiṭhnā — Try off

प्रयोग–काम को ठीक तरह से सम्भाल लो नहीं तो इस सबसे हाथ धो बैठोगे।

74. हाथ मलते रह जाना — Hāth malte rah jana — To repent

प्रयोग–अभी से संभल जाओ नहीं तो बाद में हाथ मलते रहोगे।

75. हवाई किले बनाना — Hawāi kile bananā — To build castles in the air.

प्रयोग–हवाई किले बनाने का क्या लाभ, कुछ करके दिखाओ तो जानें।

PROVERSBS लोकोक्तियाँ

1.	अँधों में काना राजा।	Aṅdhoṅ men kānā rājā	A figure among cyphers.
2.	अधजल गगरी छलकत जाये।	Adhjal gagri chhalkat jāy.	Empty vessels sound much.
3.	आप भला तो जग भला।	Āp bhalā to jag bhalā.	Good mind good find.
4.	इलाज से परहेज बेहतर।	Ilāj se parhez bahtar.	Prevention is better than cure.
5.	उतावला सो बावला।	Utavalā so bawalā.	Hurry spoils curry.
6.	एक पंथ दो काज।	Ek paṅth do kāj	To kill two birds with one stone.
7.	काम प्यारा कि चाम प्यारा।	Kām pyārā ki chām pyārā.	Handsome is that handsome does.
8.	चिराग तले अंधेरा।	Chirāg tale aṅdherā.	Nearer the church further from heaven.
9.	जब तक सांस तब तक आस।	Jabtak sāṅs tab tak ās.	While there is life there's hope.
10.	जहां फूल वहां कांटा।	Jahāṅ phūl vahāṅ kāṅṭā.	No rose without thorn.
11.	जिसकी लाठी उसकी भैंस।	Jiski lāṭhi uski bhaiṅs.	Might is right.
12.	जिसका दुख वही जाने।	Jiskā dukh vahi jāne	The wearer best knows where the shoe pinches
13.	जैसा राजा वैसी प्रजा।	Jaisā rājā vaisi prajā.	As the king so are the subjects.
14.	जैसा देश वैसा भेष।	Jaisā desh vaisā bhes.	Be a Roman when you are in Rome.

15.	जो गरजते हैं वे बरसते नहीं।	Jo garjate haiṅ ve barsate nahiṅ.	Barking dogs seldom bite.
16.	थोथा चना बाजे घना।	Thothā chanā bāje ghanā.	A little pot is soon hot.
17.	धन को धन कमाता है।	Dhan ko dhan kamātā hai.	Money begets money.
18.	नौ नगद न तेरह उधार।	Nau nakad nā terah udhar.	A bird in hand is better than two in the bush.
19.	नाच न जाने आँगन टेढ़ा।	Nāch na jane āṅgan terha.	A bad workman quarrels with the tools
20.	नीम हकीम खतरे जान।	Nim hakim khatre-jān.	A little knowledge is a dangerous thing.
21.	पानी में रहे मगर से वैर।	Pāni meṅ rahe magar se vair.	To live in Rome and strife with the Pope.
22.	बिना सेवा मेवा नहीं मिलता।	Bina sewā mewā nahiṅ milta.	No pain, no gain.
23.	मुल्ला की दौड़ मस्जिद तक।	Mullā ki dauṛ masjid tak.	The priest goes no further than the church.
24.	लोहे को लोहा काटता है।	Lohe ko lohā kaṭata hai.	Diamond cuts diamond
25.	सबसे भली चुप।	Sabse bhali chup.	Silence is golden.

•••

HINDI-ENGLISH DICTIONARY
हिंदी-अंग्रेजी शब्दकोश

Classified Glossary
वर्गीकृत शब्द सूची

1. Relations संबंधी

चाचा	Uncle
चाची	Aunt
जेठानी (देवरानी)	Sister-in-law
दादा	Grandfaher
दादी	Grandmother
दामाद	Son-in-law
नाना	Grandfather (Maternal)
नानी	Grandmother (Maternal)
पति	Husband
पत्नी	Wife
पिता	Father
पुत्र	Son
पुत्रवधू	Daughter-in-law
पुत्री	Daughter
बहन	Sister
भतीजा	Nephew
भतीजी	Niece
भाई	Brother
भांजा	Nephew
भांजी	Niece
माता	Mother
मामा	Uncle (Maternal)
मामी	Aunt (Maternal)
मौसी	Mother's sister
ससुर	Father-in-law
सास	Mother-in-law
सौतेली माँ	Step-mother

2. Domestic Articles घरेलू चीज़ें

अलमारी	Almirah
कुरसी	Chair
कैंची	Scissors
गिलास	Glass
चटाई	Mat
चमचा	Spoon

चाभी	Key
चारपाई	Bed
चूल्हा	Stove
छाता	Umbrella
टोकरी	Basket
ताला	Lock
थाली	Plate
बक्सा	Box
बर्तन	Pot
बाल्टी	Bucket
मेज	Table
मोमबत्ती	Candle
संदूक	Box
साबुन	Soap
सूई	Needle
हथौड़ी	Hammer

3. Stationery
पढ़ाई-लिखाई का सामान

अख़बार	Newspaper
आलपिन	Pin
कलम	Pen
कागज	Paper
टिकट (स्टाम्प)	Postage stamp
तार	Wire
दवात	Inkpot
नकल करने वाला पेपर	Carbon paper
नकल करने वाली पेंसिल	Copying pencil
नक्शा	Map
परकाल	Divider
पेंसिल	Pencil
पोस्टकार्ड	Postcard
फाइल	File
फीता	Tape
मोहर	Seal
रबड़	Eraser
रबड़ की मोहर	Rubber stamp
रद्दी की टोकरी	Waste-paper basket
लिफ़ाफा	Envelope
स्याही	Ink
स्याही चूस	Blotting paper

4. Parts of the body
शरीर के अंग

अँगुली (पैर)	Toe
अँगुली (हाथ)	Finger
अँगूठा (हाथ)	Thumb
आँख	Eye
ओंठ	Lip
एड़ी	Heel
कंधा	Shoulder
कमर	Waist
कान	Ear
खोपड़ी	Skull
गर्दन	Neck
गला	Throat
गाल	Cheek
घुटना	Knee
चमड़ा	Skin

चेहरा	Face
छाती (पुरुष)	Chest
छाती (स्त्री)	Breast
जांघ	Thigh
जीभ	Tongue
ठोड़ी	Chin
दाढ़ी	Beard
दाँत	Tooth
दिमाग	Brain
नस	Vein
नाक	Nose
पीठ	Back
पेट	Stomach, Belly
पेशी	Muscle
पैर	Foot
फेफड़ा	Lung
बाल	Hair
मसूड़ा	Gum
मुँह	Mouth
रीढ़	Backbone
हड्डी	Bone
हथेली	Palm
हृदय	Heart

5. Ailments रोग

कोढ़	Leprosy
कोष्ठ्बद्धता (कब्ज़)	Constipation
खांसी	Cough
गठिया	Rheumatism
गाँठ	Tumour
गूँगा	Dumb
चक्कर	Giddiness
छींक	Sneeze
ज्वर	Fever
दमा	Asthma
दाद	Ringworm
पथरी	Stone
पसीना	Sweat
पागलपन	Insanity
पीब	Pus
पीलिया	Jaundice
पेचिश	Dysentery
प्रदर	Leucorrhoea
फोड़ा	Boil
बलगम	Phelgm
बवासीर	Piles
बहुमूत्र	Diabetes
बुखार	Fever
भूख	Hunger
मूत्र	Urine
मोटापा	Fatnes
मोतिया बिंद	Cataract
रक्ताल्पता	Anaemia
लकवा	Paralysis
विष्ठा	Stool
शीतला	Small-pox
सिरदर्द	Headache
सूजन	Swelling
हैजा	Cholera

6. Clothes & Wearing वस्त्र एवं परिधान

अँगोछा	Napkin
कमीज़	Shirt

कंबल	Blanket
कोट	Coat
चादर	Sheet
जेब	Pocket
तौलियां	Towel
दस्ताने	Gloves
दुशाला	Shawl
पतलून	Pant
पायजामा	Trousers
बटन	Button
रूई	Cotton
रेशम	Silk
लंबादा	Gown
लहँगा	Petti-coat
साफ़ा (पगड़ी)	Turban

7. Ornaments आभूषण

अँगूठी	Ring
कंगन	Bracelet
कड़ा	Bangle
चूड़ी	Bangle
माला	Garland
मूंगा	Coral
मोती	Pearl
हार	Diamond

8. Flowers, Fruits & Vegetables
फल-फूल व सब्जियां

आम	Mango
आलू	Potato
अंगूर	Grape
अंजीर	Fig
ईख	Sugarcane
कमल	Lotus
कद्दू	Pumpkin
केला	Banana
खजूर	Date
गाजर	Carrot
गुलाब	Rose
घास	Grass
जामुन	Blackberry
तरबूज	Watermelon
नारियल	Coconut
नारंगी	Orange
नींबू	Lemon
पपीता	Papaya
पुदीना	Mint
पौधा	Plant
प्याज़	Onion
फूलगोभी	Cauliflower
बंद गोभी	Cabbage
बेर	Plum
बैंगन	Brinjal
मिर्च	Chilli
मूँगफली	Groundnut
मूली	Radish
लहसुन	Garlic
सेब	Apple

9. Minerals खनिज पदार्थ

कोयला	Coal
चाँदी	Silver
तांबा	Copper

पारा	Mercury
पीतल	Brass
रांगा	Tin
सीसा	Lead
लोहा	Iron

10. Cereals & Eatables
अन्न व खाद्य पदार्थ

आटा	Cornflour
कह्वा	Coffee
गेहूँ	Wheat
चना	Gram
चपाती (रोटी)	Cake
चाय	Tea
चीनी	Sugar
जौ	Barley
तेल	Oil
दही	Curd
दाल	Pulse
दूध	Milk
पनीर	Cheese
भुट्टा (मकई)	Maize
भोजन	Food
मक्खन	Butter
मलाई	Cream
मांस	Meat
मिठाई	Sweets
मुरब्बा	Jam
मैदा	Fine flour
रोटी	Bread
शक्कर	Loaf-sugar
शराब	Wine
शहद	Honey

11. Occupation व्यवसाय

अध्यापक	Teacher
कारीगर	Artisan
कलाकार	Artist
किसान	Farmer
खजांची	Treasurer
चमार (मोची)	Shoe-maker
जौहरी	Jeweller
जुलाहा	Weaver
ठठेरा	Brasier
डाकिया	Postman
डॉक्टर	Doctor
तेली	Oilman
दर्जी	Tailor
दंत चिकित्सक	Dentist
दुकानदार	Shopkeeper
धोबी	Washerman
पहरेदार	Watchman
फेरीवाला	Hawker
बढ़ई	Carpenter
भिखारी	Beggar
मछुआ	Fisherman
मल्लाह	Boatman
माली	Gardener
मुंशी	Clerk
मेहतर	Sweeper
रोकड़िया	Cashier
रंगरेज	Dyer
लेखक	Writer
वैद्य	Physician
सोनार	Goldsmith
संपादक	Editor

हलवाई	Confectioner

12. Animal पशु

ऊँट	Camel
कुत्ता	Dog
खरगोश	Rabbit
गधा	Donkey
गाय	Cow
घोड़ा	Horse
चूहा	Mouse
दुम	Tail
पशु	Beas
पंजा	Claw
पिल्ला	Puppy
बकरा	He-goat
बकरी	She-goat
बछड़ा	Calf
बिल्ली	Cat
बंदर	Monkey
बैल	Ox
भालू	Bear
भेड़	Sheep
मेमना	Lamb
लोमड़ी	Fox
साँड	Bull
सियार	Jackal
सिंह	Lion
सूअर	Pig
हिरण	Deer
हाथी	Elephant

13. Birds पक्षी

अंडा	Egg
उल्लू	Owl
कबूतर	Pigeon
कोयल	Cuckoo
कौआ	Crow
गरुड़	Eagle
गौरइया	Sparrow
घोंसला	Nest
चमगादड़	Bat
चील	Kite
चोंच	Beak
डैना	Wing
पिंजड़ा	Cage
बुलबुल	Nightingale
मुर्गा	Cock
मुर्गी	Hen
मोर	Peacock
सारस	Crane
हंस	Swan

SOME IMPORTANT HINDI VERBS
कुछ प्रमुख हिंदी क्रियाएँ

अकुलाना	to feel uneasy.	उमड़ना	to overflow
अटकना	to be held up	उलझना	to be entangled
अलसाना	to feel lazy	उलटना	to overturn
आना	to come	ऊँघना	to doze
इतराना	to behave in self conceited manner.	ऐंठना	to twist
		ओढ़ना	to cover the body
		कड़कना	to crackle
उकसाना	to provoke	कतरना	to cut
उखड़ना	to be dislocated	कमाना	to earn
उखाड़ना	to dislocate	करना	to do
उगना	to grow	कसना	to tighten
उगलना	to talk out	कहना	to say
उचटना	to withdraw from	काँपना	to tremble
उछलना	to jump	खटकना	to pinch
उजड़ना	to be ruined	खाना	to eat
उजाड़ना	to ruin	खिजाना	to tease
उठना	to raise	खेलना	to play
उठाना	to lift up	गँवाना	to waste
उड़ाना	to fly	गाना	to sing
उतरना	to get down	गिनना	to count
उतारना	to unload	गिरना	to fall
उधेड़ना	to unsew	गिराना	to cause to fall
उभरना	to bulge out	गुजरना	to pass

गुर्राना	to growl	निभाना	to carry on
घुसना	to enter	पकड़ना	to catch
घूमना	to wander	पचना	to be digested
घेरना	to encircle	पटकना	to throw down
घोलना	to dissolve	पढ़ना	to read
चकराना	to feel dizzy	पधारना	to arrive
चखना	to taste	पहनना	to wear
चढ़ना	to rise	पालना	to bring up
चलना	to walk	पीटना	to beat
चमकना	to shine	पीसना	to grind
चाटना	to lick	पुकारना	to call
चाहना	to wish	पैठना	to enter
चुराना	to steal	पोंछना	to wipe
छीनना	to snatch	फँसना	to be entrapped
धुड़ाना	to get released	फटकारना	to rebuke
जाना	to go	फाड़ना	to torn
जानना	to know	फिरना	to go round
जीतना	to win	फूलना	to swell
जोतना	to plough	फेंकना	to throw
झगड़ना	quarrel	बकना	to chatter
झूलना	to swing	बढ़ना	to increase
टहलना	to stroll	बताना	to tell
टालना	to postpone	बदलना	to change
डालना	to put in	बनाना	to make
ढकना	to cover	बरसना	to rain
तरसना	to long for	बिगाड़ना	to spoil
ताड़ना	to guess	बैठना	to sit
तोड़ना	to break	बोलना	to speak
थमना	to stop	भड़काना	to be exited
दौड़ना	to run	भागना	to run
धिक्कारना	to curse	माँगना	to demand
निकालना	to take out	मोड़ना	to turn
निबाहना	to maintain	रखना	to put

रचना	to make
रटना	to memorize
रहना	to live
रोकना	to stop
लगना	to appear
लगाना	to engage
लटकना	to hang
लपेटना	to fold
लाँघना	to cross
लादना	to load
लिखना	to write
लेना	to get
लौटना	to return
वारना	to sacrifice
विचारना	to think
सँजोना	to arrange
सजाना	to decorate
सड़ना	to decay
सींचना	irrigate
सीखना	to learn
सीना	to stich
सुनना	to hear
सूखना	to dry up
सूझना	to occur to one's mind
सौंपना	to hand over
हँसना	to laugh
हँसाना	to amuse
हकलाना	to stammer
हड़पना	to swallow
हथियाना	to seize
हाँफना	to pant
हारना	to lose
हिलना	to be moved
दिखना	to be seen
देखना	to see
दोहराना	to revise

BOOKS ON SELF-HELP

Rs 150/-

SUCCESS MANTRA (Sh. Joginder Singh)

This book is a masterpiece by Sh. Joginder Singh, IPS (Retd) who is a former Director of the CBI. Hailing from a poor farmer's family, he scaled the pinnacles of success through sheer motivation and hard work. The saga of success he has enunciated through his win-win story is worth emulating for any young aspirant for achievements and glory in life: to be on top!

HOW TO EXCEL WHEN CHIPS ARE DOWN

(Sh. Joginder Singh)

Rs 95/-

Excellent suggestions with suitable examples have been cited in the book which will guide youngesters about the importance of objective thinking and to erase unwanted thoughts from their memory.

Rs 150/-

FOR A BETTER TOMORROW (Sh. Joginder Singh)

This magnum opus by Sh. Joginder Singh is a treatise on self improvement. This win-win sory is based on the secrets of success as to how to become an achiever. And the success mantra that he espouses for you. Make the best of all opportunities; dream big and work hard- dreams will turn sheer realities.

WINNING WAYS

(Sh. Joginder Singh)

Rs 150/-

The mantra he unveils for success, through this book, is potent enough to lift the young and ambitious to the highest peaks. These winning tips will inspire your morale to achieve greater glories - you simply need to tune up your mindset and hone your skills.

Rs 95/-

DISCOVERY OF INDEPENDENT INDIA

By: Joginder Singh (Former CBI Director)

Violation of human rights does not occur only at the hands of the enforcement agencies. Rampant corruption in Govt. department will whom a citizen comes across at the cutting edge level, tell their own story. The biggest hurdle which inhibits the citizen from coming forward to help the police is the deplorable condition prevailing in the Court of law.

TURN YOUR CREATIVE SPARK INTO A FLAME

Joginder Singh

Rs 95/-

This book explains the significance of motivating today's youngesters and other aspirants on various aspects. It acts as an eye-opener about the common mistakes that everyone commit in their lives, that is badly managing the schedules and wastage of the precious time of our life.